THE BOOK OF
DALLAS

PHOTOGRAPHS BY
BOB SMITH AND LAURA GARZA

Introduction by ERIK JONSSON

THE BOOK OF

DALLAS

Edited by

EVELYN OPPENHEIMER
and
BILL PORTERFIELD

DOUBLEDAY & COMPANY, INC.

GARDEN CITY, NEW YORK

1976

The selection from "The Church in Dallas"
by Lewis Chamberlain is reprinted,
with permission, from *Theology Today,*
Vol. XXVI, No. 2, July 1969.

Library of Congress Cataloging in Publication Data
Main entry under title: THE BOOK OF DALLAS.
1. Dallas—Addresses, essays, lectures.
I. Oppenheimer, Evelyn, 1907–   II. Porterfield, Bill.
F394.D2B66 1976   976.4'2812
ISBN 0-385-11403-6

Library of Congress Catalog Card Number 76-2811
BOOK DESIGN BY BENTE HAMANN
First Edition after the Limited Edition of 250 copies

Contents

Preface

by EVELYN OPPENHEIMER

I was born and grew up in Dallas and I inherited the psyche of the city, whatever that intangible is.

Not all cities develop an urban personality; some do, but for very different reasons. Obvious reasons may come from geography, just the physical location on a coast or lake or river which gives the city the atmosphere and commercial advantage of a port. More subtle reasons for a city's distinction are those entirely man-made. The spirit of Dallas, which has attracted men and women and resulted in such phenomenal growth and metropolitan reputation, is in this latter class. As an old-timer said, "It is man's *yes* to God's *no*."

Dallas is set on a north Texas plain or prairie. Latitude 32°47′, longitude 96°48′, elevation 512. Nothing of scenic note is adjacent. The inconspicuous Trinity River has made news only by flooding at times. Visions of its navigability have remained visions. So what has made Dallas?

What has brought some 940,000 people into its city limits of 296 square miles and a 2,700,000 population into what is now the tenth largest metro and marketing area in the nation? What has made it the high-ranking headquarters center nationally for 204 insurance companies as well as publicly held corporations and million-dollar-plus companies? What has made it a leading fashion, gift, and home furnishings center with a market attracting 200,000 buyers a year and a gross annual sales total of $2.5 billion? What has brought official representatives of twenty-six foreign countries here? What has built 102 hospitals and clinics and eight medical research education institutions? What has put Dallas into the top five convention and exposition centers in the United States? What has made 131 Planned Industrial Districts covering some 24,000 acres of land? What attracts over two million tourists a year? What built multiple radio and television stations? What created an airport bigger than Manhattan Island? What, we repeat, has made Dallas?

Men and women have. Railroad tracks did. Astute handling of money and credit to produce and market cotton, cattle, and later oil and to distribute goods and provide services. Ranches, blackland cotton farms, and gins and mills got Dallas financing. Oil exploration, drilling, and equipment got more of the same. Money was the generator, but a sense of commitment was part of the capital, the gamble, the investment.

People have a special pride when they build something out of nothing, and so civic pride evolved into another generating force. With money, people wanted things. They also wanted more of the culture they had brought with them or read and heard about. Society was to adorn business, as it has and did and does. The vitality of progress in terms of profit was homogenized with conservative philosophy.

As a native old enough to have childhood memories of the Old Dallas to which my parents had come as bride and groom from Missouri and Illinois in 1900, and now as a citizen of New Dallas, I have shared both the tingle and the trauma of the city's pride in what is done and not done and in what is magnetic attraction to people who come to what they call Big D from other places.

It was the same in my father's day and generation when Big D was very little. What made a young man at the turn of the century choose this town to settle in and to open a business? I remember him saying once that he had felt the same promise of growth in young Dallas as in young Detroit. I remember hearing that pioneer merchant E. M. Kahn once said that he settled in Dallas in 1872 because "the men walked faster here."

The majority of men who turned the town into a city were not sons of the Old South. They were not used to having their work done for them. They came from the North and East, and many were immigrants from the Old World who had the motivation of natural necessity and the vigor of the pioneer concept: freedom to get what you wanted and to be and to do what you dreamed. But the women they married were more often of traditional background, and they added a cultural seasoning to what was new and robust in a community where money did the talking.

The turn of the century saw annual editions of Blue Books of Society printed in Dallas to satisfy social vanity and Chamber of Commerce promotion. It all went together in a way voiced by a young banker who was later Mayor Robert L. Thornton, Sr.: "Keep the dirt flying!" It was a motto of compulsive growth. It put drama into statistics.

There is this quality in Dallas, something that excites the imagination and builds an aggressive confidence. It made a natural liaison with the independence indigenous to Texas and the Southwest.

None of this can be defined simply, as nothing can be that emanates from a human complex geared to establishment, yet keyed to frontier spirit. Mink and boots, Rembrandts and Remingtons may seem to be contradictory tastes, but they can be complementary and are in Dallas.

Born in Dallas, Evelyn Oppenheimer is a graduate of the University of Chicago, Phi Beta Kappa. Her professional career has been mainly in book reviewing, conducting the oldest book program on radio in the United States and now broadcast in Dallas, Houston, Phoenix, Los Angeles, and San Francisco with Doubleday Book Shops as sponsor. She has taught special courses in reviewing at the University of Texas in Austin, Texas Technological University, the University of California in Los Angeles, the University of Dallas, Southern Methodist University, and the University of Wisconsin Extension. She is also a literary agent and the author of books on Americana, public speaking, and reviewing. She has received the Matrix Award in the field of cultural communication from the Dallas Chapter of Theta Sigma Phi.

Bill Porterfield writes for newspapers, magazines, radio, and television. Born in East Texas and reared in South Texas, he has moved about mid-America, working, he says, for the best publications and the worst. He has been on the staff of the New Braunfels *Zeitung,* the Houston *Chronicle,* the Detroit *Free Press,* and the Chicago *Daily News,* and he has written for *The New York Times Sunday Magazine,* the now defunct New York *Herald Tribune, The Christian Science Monitor,* World Book Encyclopedia Science Service, *The Saturday Evening Post,* the *Texas Monthly,* the *Texas Observer,* and *D Magazine.* Presently, Porterfield is appearing on *Newsroom,* a production of KERA-TV 13, the public television station in Dallas. He has written, produced, and narrated films that have been shown over the Public Broadcasting Service.

In 1963 Porterfield won the Ernie Pyle Memorial Award, given by Scripps-Howard Newspapers, and he is a two-time winner of the Texas Institute of Letters' Stanley Walker Award. He became, in 1967, the first writing fellow at J. Frank Dobie's Paisano Ranch, a retreat for the creative sponsored by the University of Texas and the Texas Institute of Letters. He is the author of the book *LBJ Country* and has been published in several anthologies.

Preface

by BILL PORTERFIELD

I came to Dallas with reluctance and I remain with enthusiasm. This, of course, reflects as much of me as it does the city. I have accommodated myself to local eccentricities, and Dallas in turn has made some room for mine. In the exchange I have found a place for myself, which surprises, for I did not expect it when I came. My experience is not unique nor is it the rule, but I think it reflects the feeling of most newcomers to Dallas, no matter where they come from or what notions they bring with them. The city is mature enough now to be fairly democratic and flexible in its attitude toward exotics, and while we are hardly a New York or a San Francisco or even a San Antonio, we are not the Dallas of November 22, 1963.

I said I came here with reluctance. That is because I came after the assassination, six years after the frightful fact, full of prejudices and preconceptions, and yet somehow fascinated by the prospect. If I had come before the fact, say in the 1950s as a fledgling reporter from South Texas, I would have come not with reluctance but with reverence, as a rude outlander to Rome. For then Dallas was, in John Gunther's words, "a true metropolis . . . packed with charm." Where else in Texas or the Southwest could you find such hotels and restaurants, so many stunning stores, and such a well-endowed arts life? Circumstances, however, saw me to Houston, a raw, unruly place where the people, in their hybrid vigor, were both contemptuous and jealous of the chic that Dallas radiated. Through the years, I watched both places grow and change according to their character. Dallas is an inland city and tended to attract men who were inward-looking. Its patriarchs were heroic in their dreams for Dallas, but once they had satisfied themselves they tended to draw up the bridges of the Trinity River moat and fend off outsiders. The inlander is by nature conservative, like the European of old. Eric Hoffer has the sense of it, in his 1963 book, *The Ordeal of Change:*

When on rare occasions one of the lowly had reached the top in Europe he had kept the pattern intact and, if anything, tightened the screws. The stuffy little corporal from Corsica harnessed the lusty forces released by the French Revolution to a gilded state coach, and could think of nothing grander than mixing his blood with that of the Hapsburg masters and establishing a new dynasty, re-establishing and reinforcing the old pattern.

That was Hoffer on Napoleon, but it could as well be Warren Leslie on Uncle Bob Thornton and the Dallas oligarchy, better known as the old Dallas Citizens Council. The old bulls who built Dallas closed the community politically to all save those who could afford noblesse oblige. Refinements and image—entrenchment— became more important than the give and take that would occur in a more open city. In a sense, our bankers made of the city a vault, and along in the late fifties and early sixties, Dallas experienced atrophy and an almost pathological reaction to change.

Houston, on the other hand, was a coastal city. Or almost. They made it one by digging a channel fifty miles to the Gulf. Men who settle at the edge of continents, close to waterways, are looking for company, whatever the traffic will bear. It takes a certain kind of backbone to go inland and carve out a fort for yourself in the wilderness, and it takes a different kind of guts to set yourself up as a port to take on all comers. That's what the Houston men did.

A port is a place of flux, of movement, not entrenchment. Liquid. Men come and go. You don't care where they come from or where they are going, you just interact, on a business basis. And sometimes you even get social. Commodities may change, and modes of transportation, but a port is a port, a place for adventure and opportunity. The word gets around that things are happening in Houston, and men who want to make things happen tend to navigate toward a place like that. Self-perpetuating prophecy. And as a place like Houston grows and adapts to new demands and technology, the kinds of adventurers it attracts change. The impulse and vigor is the same if the manner is different. The boom goes on. The buccaneers keep coming, first a Laffite and then a Hofheinz.

In a word, Houston drew the adventurer. Dallas didn't. The one became a place for men to make money and the other a place for men to keep their wealth.

And then, one fall Friday, three shots in Dealey Plaza changed Dallas' image from Gunther's charming metropolis to the Warren Commission's "atmosphere of hate." A metamorphosis was inevitable, and it took place.

Oh, some things would never change. There would always be the State Fair and the Cotton Bowl, and Stanley Marcus would continue to cater to the rich and instruct them in the art of elegant and conspicuous consumption, while down the street Brother W. A. Criswell carried on in the world's largest Baptist church, passing the collection to twenty thousand believers. In football, finery, and fundamentalism, Dallas would not only endure but prevail.

But beneath those civic costumes, important changes took place. This is not to say that Dallas has undergone a miraculous transformation and is on all accounts an open and democratic American city. Sometimes it seems to take one step forward and two backward. In this it is much like any other American city, in that the same forces for change are at work. But there is one important exception, and this is that violence has not erupted seriously here since the assassination. The tendency toward revolution and reaction is somehow subdued. The people of Dallas, whatever their color and complaint, seem to have learned patience and tolerance, to live with the travail of these times with more hope than hatred and bitterness.

Today, it seems to be one of the saner American cities, where the old and established and the new and active exchange their give and take in a gradual and civil manner. And we are hardly in the doldrums. In our own electronic and abstract way we are growing, looking outward and welcoming the world again. And with the new airport we have taken our fort and made of it a port, to match Houston's!

Bob Smith is a Methodist minister, a pilot, and a prize-winning photojournalist. Born in the Oak Cliff section of Dallas, Smith earned a B.A. at Southern Methodist University and an M.A. at Perkins School of Theology. A pastor for five years, he turned to photography and the Dallas *Morning News,* where he won four Dallas Press Club "Katies" for his work. He and his wife teamed as free-lancers in 1974 and have had their work published here and abroad.

Laura Garza established her reputation as a photographer with KERA-TV 13, the Dallas public television station, where she developed a photo-essay style that won her a gold medal in the international Atlanta Film Festival. Born in Austin, Ms. Garza studied art at Texas Woman's University and archaeology at the National University of Mexico. A free-lancer now, Ms. Garza, like her husband, Bob Smith, is a licensed pilot and often flies into the jungles of Central and South America to photograph pre-Columbian ruins and artifacts. Smith and Garza are members of the American Society of Magazine Photographers.

THE BOOK OF
DALLAS

Paterfamilias of his adopted city, Erik Jonsson came to Dallas in 1934. He was born in Brooklyn in 1901.

Mr. Jonsson holds the M.E. degree from Rensselaer Polytechnic Institute, honorary degrees from seven other universities, the Founders Medal of the National Academy of Engineers, the Hoover Medal, and the Gantt Medal, and he was elected to the Hall of Fame for Business Leadership in 1975.

Former president and chairman of the board of Texas Instruments, Inc., he is now a director and honorary chairman of the board. For fifteen years he served as a director of Equitable Life Assurance Society of the United States and is a director of Republic National Bank of Dallas and associate director of Citizens State Bank of Richardson.

In civic leadership, Mr. Jonsson was mayor of Dallas from 1964 to 1971, president of the Chamber of Commerce and Dallas Citizens Council, and originator of the Goals for Dallas program. He was first chairman of the board of the Dallas–Fort Worth Regional Airport.

The Jonsson philanthropies in the educational and medical fields are on the largest scale. A founder of the Southwest Center for Advanced Studies, which became the University of Texas at Dallas, he is also a trustee of colleges and universities from Texas to New England. He is a member of the Visiting Committee of the School of Business of Harvard University and the Board of Visitors at Tulane University.

Mr. Jonsson is married to the former Margaret Elizabeth Fonde, of Mobile, Alabama.

Dallas: An Introduction

by ERIK JONSSON

I am sentimental about Dallas. I expect to remain so until the end of my days and I offer no apologies for that. The reasons for my feelings are many and varied, as I shall try to explain, but they stem principally from my assessment of our people—friendly, sturdy, reliable self-starters who ask no odds of anyone. They have provided ample proof that they are what I first thought them to be—reasonable, straightforward citizens whose handshake in agreement is often as good or better than a formal contract.

I pretend to be neither a trained historian nor a skilled writer, simply one who chanced to be near the center of the action here. What follows is an effort to illuminate the reasons why for more than forty years I have thought of this city, not just as a place to live, but as "home."

I believe the tremendous growth of Dallas and its environs in recent years didn't just happen; it came about because open-minded innovative people created opportunities that might have lain fallow without their recognition of those assets other than natural resources that were present here. Doggedly determined and persistent in their efforts, they cheerfully made up for lack of nature's blessings with hard work and the kind of ingenuity for which the Connecticut Yankees of two hundred years ago were renowned. Texans brought up on ranches and farms, I have found, can make things work better with a few "oddments"—with baling wire, string, and imagination—than those better trained and equipped but lacking their ingenuity. No one, to my knowledge, has ever accused a Texan of lacking imagination!

It has often been said of Dallas that there is really no valid reason for its existence, located as it is without the rich nearby natural resources that usually spawn cities. Instead, its people created the city's major asset: a network of railroads, highways, and airlines that makes our city the same kind of transportation hub in the Southwest that Chicago affords in the north-central area. More federal highways intersect here than anywhere else in the country, eight rail lines serve the area, and presently even more important, many trunk and feeder airlines use Dallas as an interchange point for destinations anywhere in the world. Excellent access and transportation have furthered the business aims of venturesome, trade-minded people from the city's beginnings, and largely shaped its destiny. Thus Dallas was pointed early toward the distribution of goods to the Southwest, later to a much wider area. This in turn led to the development of large, strong banks to finance growing commerce and a mushrooming manufacturing industry that evolved from the great production efforts of World War II.

A brief of the foregoing could well be a recipe for sound, rapid growth and development of a metropolitan center, one that becomes a magnet for headquarters, major divisions, and branches of the great corporations of our country:

Take good people who are willing to work hard for fair pay and the opportunity to do better,

Add quick and easy access to large markets near and far,

Sprinkle with strong, able, and adequate banking institutions,

Temper with a superb climate nine or ten months of the year (though hot and dry in July and August),

Season with pleasant and profitable dealings in a community that hasn't forgotten how to smile.

But I wander! It is my aim to construct no market-basket list of business goodies for the reader, though I could. Rather I should like to create a feeling for the reasons why this ancient one, born a "damyankee" in Brooklyn, raised in northern New Jersey, sparks so strongly to Texas in general and Dallas in particular. For me it begins with my first visit to Big D in the fall of 1930.

I was then a recently employed mechanical engineer (in charge of a small laboratory in Newark, New Jersey) whose function was to design and build sensitive but rugged instruments and equipment for use in exploring for oil and gas. The firm was Geophysical Service, Inc., and its two principal officers were John Clarence Karcher and Eugene McDermott. "Karch" asked me to come to Texas for ten days to observe how the instruments were used in the field, so that I might improve them. The invitation was welcome, for at that time I had never been much farther south or west than Knoxville, Tennessee.

My first impression of Dallas as I emerged from its Union Station into bright sunlight was of fresh, clean air and white buildings unmarred by the soot so commonplace in the East. The southeast breeze was a balmy zephyr that September day, pretty girls were in crisp cotton dresses, men in neat summer clothes—all looked clean, competent, and assured. When I stopped in a drugstore for cigarettes, an attractive young lady supplied them, made change, smiled, and said "Hurry

back" as though she really meant it. There was nothing like that where I came from!

In the following week I traveled through much of Oklahoma and East Texas, encountering unvarying courtesy and kindness. I observed many farmers and ranchers out in the country using new farm equipment, new trucks, busily working. Obviously the Depression wasn't getting *them* down. To my comments along this line the replies all carried the same tone: "It's a little rough, so we'll just have to work harder to get through it."

Returning to New Jersey, I remarked to my wife, Margaret: "I've seen the place where I'd like to live, work, and watch our children grow up healthy and strong in a climate ideal for outdoor living. Will you trust my judgment and risk a move there if the chance comes our way?" "Any time," she replied (a natural answer, after all, for one who was born in Mobile and had spent her early years moving to Alabama, Mississippi, and Tennessee).

In April 1934 we were on our way to Dallas. Soon I was given the GSI title of "Office Manager," a job with many and varied responsibilities—thus beginning a succession of years in which I had a great chance to learn management techniques and practices. These years also blessed me with the opportunity to meet, observe, and know Dallas leaders as they pursued their careers, pushed their institutions to higher levels, carried their city ahead with them. That experience matched my first observations: Dallas folks were competitive but fair-minded, decent, and kind. Socially or in business, I found people to respect. Risk was no stranger to them, adversity something to be overcome every day.

As the depression-ridden thirties gave way to the war and recovery days of the 1940s, Dallas burgeoned—blossomed—with plentiful opportunities, ultimately to become not only a banking and distribution center but a sophisticated manufacturing city, with special emphasis on technical industries such as aircraft, missiles, and electronics. Good labor conditions prevailed; companies and their people prospered. Taxes were kept low and the city was honestly and efficiently run under a city-manager form of government.

The four largest banks, headed by men of vision and competence, had grown too, and stood high in national rankings. With their aid, concern, and understanding, other business and community institutions matured in admirable ways. Dallas, as well as Texas, was developing at a phenomenal rate, and emigration, particularly from the North and East, brought new residents, new plants, and new businesses in numbers that at times threatened to swamp the city's capacity to absorb them. The transportation facilities to support the new flood of activities developed as well, with commercial, business, and private aviation beginning to play an important part as flying became commonplace. The weather, extremely favorable for air transportation, made possible the maintenance of highly reliable schedules.

Dallasites took to the aerial mode easily and naturally, using airplanes to span the gaps between Texas towns and the great cities of the world, establishing new business ties, a new social consciousness, a new cosmopolitan outlook. If their orientation and the rapidity of change forced them to overlook comparable development of some facets of the finer cultural aspects of their lives, no matter, they would "catch up on them" later. Indeed, their over-all accomplishments in the span of a few decades were nothing short of remarkable.

I recite these facts not simply to project a picture of growth and prosperity, but rather to bring forward and speak about Dallas' spirit—the strong fraternal ties that exist among so many of our townsmen, the reason why they and I think and speak of Dallas as "our town." It is a good place. Pictures or descriptions of its physical setting cannot transmit the feelings most of us have about it—the pleasure of living and working each day among people who enjoy sharing an environment with others they like, respect, and admire. Some may dismiss this as "local pride," but in truth it is tangible and real, leading to joint achievements otherwise impossible.

An eleven-year-old program involving Dallas citizens in matters of mutual concern characterizes this point, and I should like to describe it from the personal viewpoint of my own involvement and how it came about.

By the 1960s I had come to the chairmanship of a successful technologically oriented company headquartered here. My company, Texas Instruments, was now large, widely known, and listed on the New York Stock Exchange. Preparing for gradual retirement, I began to take on some civic jobs, such as the Chamber of Commerce presidency, while looking forward to half-time work and extensive travel with my family when I reached age sixty. That was not to be.

In 1963 I was elected president of the Dallas Citizens Council, an organization of businessmen whose only purpose was and is to endorse useful local projects, with members assisting in their necessary financing and accomplishment. John Connally, whom I knew only slightly at the time, was then governor of Texas. He advised the Citizens Council of President Kennedy's desire to come to Texas and asked it to sponsor a Dallas luncheon for the President. The disaster that followed is history, although not yet as accurately told as I should like. In many places around the world we became known as a "city of hate"—a city that killed a president instead of one in which a president was killed by a political radical and possible psychopath. His counterparts may be found anywhere, as we knew then and others now realize.

What followed were days and months of review, probing, exacting self-examination. Outside criticism came close to wholesale indictment and outright damnation of a whole community by a large part of the world. As decent citizens who had done all they could to make the President welcome and safe (he was *our* President, too) we were stunned and hurt, and a few were bitter. The bitterness, however, did not last. All knew we must regroup and start anew—we had neither time nor inclination for recriminations.

In February 1964 the mayor of Dallas, Earle Cabell, became ineligible to continue his duties after announcing his decision to run for a congressional seat. Rather than

selecting one of their own members to succeed him, the remaining eight members of the Dallas City Council invited me to accept an appointment to the fifteen-month remainder of his term—to nobody's surprise more than mine. I accepted, and was elected to three additional two-year terms as well. In many another city I might have become just another neophyte devoured by political wolves. Here, once again, I found new ways to value the help and support of Dallasites and their institutions.

For the initial period of my new job as mayor, I was busy to the point of saturation with the duties and the required learning implicit in the oath of office—"to preserve, protect, and defend. . . ." That phrase moved me profoundly, somewhat to my surprise, and kept coming to mind whenever matters weren't going well. The words seemed to haunt and drive me to do more, for whatever was accomplished never seemed to be enough.

I had no political background beyond that of the ordinary citizen, and found the work fascinating, taxing, and challenging. Yet for months I felt like one on a treadmill, getting nowhere, until one day I awoke to the fact that I was not applying properly the basic business and management principles learned over a lifetime. The people in City Hall were hard-working, conscientious, honest, and decent. The trouble in getting things done lay with the way they and their tasks were organized and in the short-term orientation in which nearly all policies were constrained in the strait jacket of one-year budgets. "Get with it," I told myself. "Don't you remember how to set goals, plan for their achievement, estimate costs, measure resources, set priorities, and all the rest?"

Shortly thereafter I proposed to a downtown civic club audience that we construct a team to take inventory of Dallas' condition in a dozen of the most important categories of mutual concern to our people and to follow this with a convocation of representative citizens to consider what our goals should be. The goals categories were set: Government of the City; Design of the City; Health; Welfare; Transportation; Public Safety; Elementary and Secondary Education; Higher Education; Continuing Education; Cultural Activities; Recreation and Entertainment; the Economy of Dallas.

The convocation was held—in historic Salado, Texas, 130 miles south of Dallas. Goals were drafted, consensus reached, and the results were published and submitted for approval or negation by Dallas citizens. This was followed by twenty-six neighborhood meetings covering every part of town to discuss the goals. Attendance ranged from fifty to six hundred people at each. They made suggestions and changes; these were incorporated and a second volume was published, broadly circulated, and studied. We then began to organize plans, priorities, and schedules for achieving the goals.

We called the program Goals for Dallas. To all of us who took part, it presented a marvelous opportunity to get acquainted and exchange viewpoints with literally thousands of our fellow citizens—from all walks of life, of all ethnic, racial, and religious varieties, and all levels of educational, social, and economic backgrounds.

It provided every citizen with a chance to express orally or in written form what he believed our city should be like in years to come. As one black woman said to me following our first convocation: "Today I had a voice. Today I felt that I *was* an American." That remark thrilled all who heard it. It gave confirmation to my belief that we had structured a new form of participative democracy, one in which people instructed their institutions, public and private, as to their needs and desires, reversing previous custom.

Goals for Dallas has been characterized by an open-ended continuing cycle of thoughtful, pointed gathering of information about ourselves and our city, and deliberations and decision-making involving as many citizens as could be enlisted. It was not just that anyone *could* participate but that *all* were sought, invited, and urged to do so. The inviolable principle has been that the goals and the methods for reaching them should be decided by the *people* of Dallas themselves. The program has been kept nonpartisan, nonpolitical, and independent. It has not been a governmental process, but a process shared by people free to choose.

A goals program informs and involves the citizens, correlates and communicates the people's wishes, to public and private organizations charged with specific functions in the city, causing these to be more responsive. Likewise, when the people have expressed their views, firmly and clearly, support of worthwhile undertakings usually follows.

It would be fair to ask, however, if sufficient gains are made in the quality of community life to justify the time, trouble, and expense involved in goal setting and planning. The answer that comes back from those now engaged in revising, updating, and expanding the goals set a decade ago is a resounding yes.

Gathering information about a city's problems, its condition, and its needs and the communication of these to all, together with evaluation and commentary on proposed decision-making and actions by a credible, substantial cross section of the citizenry results in raising the sights and ambitions of all. To be specific, Dallas' 1967 capital appropriations program for needed improvements was $350 million to be spread over three years, or roughly $117 million annually. This approximately tripled the previous rate. The bond issue was overwhelmingly approved at the polls in a year when even school bond elections were being roundly defeated in the Southeast and Southwest. Many of these improvements are now complete. They include a new Municipal Services Center, many attractive new branch libraries, an expanded convention center, the nation's largest airport, and numerous others.

Less tangible, but probably more valuable, is the strengthening of ties among people which leads them to discuss problems and reach mutually acceptable solutions in a peaceful and civilized manner based on common knowledge and understanding. Laymen observe local governmental and private institutions striving to implement programs that they themselves have asked for, and co-operation becomes a substitute for complaints.

Dallas has an Action Center at City Hall. It is designed to make obsolete the old cliché "You can't fight City Hall." Its purpose is to encourage citizens to bring appropriate problems there and be met with courtesy, consideration, and a cheerful "We'll help if we can."

A decade after 108 goals in twelve mutual areas of concern were set by more than 100,000 citizens, many of whom were of high school and college age, some 125,000 copies of six published Goals for Dallas books have been distributed locally. Five thousand more have been sent on request to cities, counties, and states both here and abroad.

It is estimated that 27 per cent of all goals have been completed, 43 per cent show substantial progress, 28 per cent moderate progress, and 2 per cent no progress. Their range is from physical facilities such as those mentioned earlier to social and health services in disadvantaged areas.

How we expend our resources of time, energy, money, and materials in the cities can determine the fate of America. How well we expend our resources will depend on our awareness of what *can* be done and our wisdom in choosing what *should* be done. Continuous constructive innovation bearing directly on deeply instilled, often archaic customs is one of the ingredients needed most in local governments. The catalyst that most often brings this about is the inventive, inquiring mind of the young person who doesn't know he or she can't do something and therefore tries and does it. We in the cities need to tap this constructive force, as well as every other existing resource.

More important, we shall need to have at the heart of every innovation and technological application a deep and abiding concern for the propriety and the effect of the changes we impose on human beings, for we live in an environment so totally different from any previously faced by man that the old ideas of how to get along just won't do.

Too often we only *react* to change and events as they occur rather than *acting* to control those that are bound to happen and can be foreseen. Instead, we should determine that we will *design* the future rather than allow the future to impose a design on us for our way of life. In Goals for Dallas the narrow view of expediency has been replaced by fuller realization of the need to survey all community problems and give proper weight to each in reaching solutions.

When I proposed the program more than a decade ago, this is what I wrote about it in my city: "As one who grew up in New York, then the world's largest city, I am totally unimpressed with the phenomenon of great size. Quality of a community, however, is something else. It is this quality, this excellence, which led me to bring my family to Texas and to Dallas more than thirty years ago. It is this quality, this excellence, which I still see shining forth in our whole Southwest, that makes me wish to stay and be a part of it. The Goals proposal seems to me to provide the framework within which we can understand more about what has brought us to our present level of accomplishment and quality and what can make it possible for us to understand it and thus to enhance it further.

"In time, I think we shall be a community known not only for its size, its spaciousness, its cleanliness, its tall buildings, or its other physical characteristics, but rather as an aggregation of strong, independent people, who understand their destiny and want to march toward it with vigor and determination. I care not at all whether Dallas becomes the United States' largest city. What I wish Dallas to be in the future is what in the past I have believed it to be: the *best* city in the United States."

Fate and the winds of change and of chance will have a lot to do with that. Greatness does not come easily to a city, nor can it be accomplished without the vision, the desire, the diligence, and the durability of its people. The challenge is clear and of a kind to which Dallas' citizens have risen in the past. Much has been accomplished. Much remains to be done.

What will the future be like? Will it be fair and pleasant or stormy and rough? A fair measure of both, I hope, for man, as does steel, needs tempering.

The fires of adversity will be around for a long time. We here in Dallas must deal with the same spectrum of problems and ailments common to all large cities—slums, crime, unemployment, inflation, urban decay, and more. These obstacles to the enjoyment of community peace, progress, and prosperity are formidable, but not insuperable. My faith is unlimited that leaders will be on hand to cope with them.

My crystal ball is cloudy on specific, physical things, but on Dallas and Texas there is a certain rosy glow. Once I wrote: ". . . Most of all a city is people. It is not just a place *for* people; it *is* people." With few exceptions those among whom I live size up remarkably well. I am proud to be with them and for them—and I commend them and *their* city to the reader with all my heart.

DALLAS TRADEMARKS
AND SYMBOLS

OPPOSITE: Big Tex, at the State Fair grounds.
OVERLEAF: The Flying Red Horse atop the Mobil Building (formerly the Magnolia Building). In the foreground is the Adolphus Hotel.
PAGE 18: The John F. Kennedy Memorial.
PAGE 20: The Dallas Cowboys.
PAGE 23: At the opera.

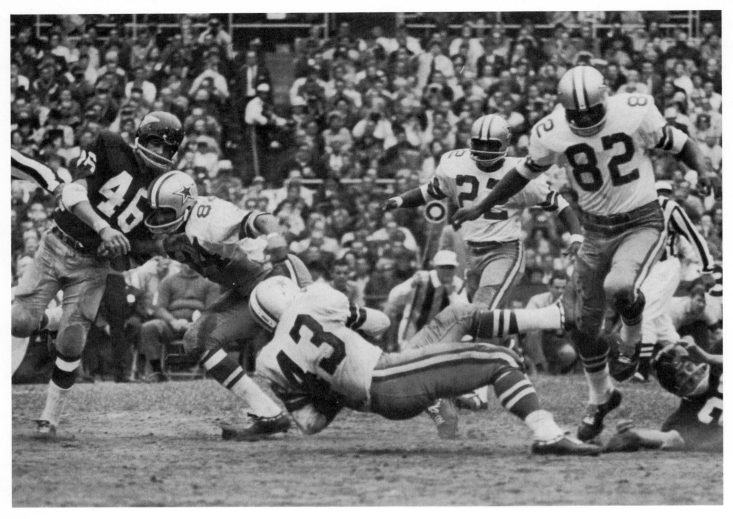

LONGHORN
Ballroom
THUR NITE OCT 2
WILLIE NELSON
DEWEY WED THRU SUN LONNIE
GROOM GILL

Named one of the Ten Outstanding Young Men of America and one of the Five Outstanding Young Texans in 1970, also the Outstanding Young Man of Dallas the previous year, Walter J. Humann holds a B.S. degree from Massachusetts Institute of Technology, a Master of Business Administration degree from Harvard, and the Doctorate of Jurisprudence from Southern Methodist University Evening Law School.

Born in Dallas in 1937, his career has included the vice-presidency of LTV Corporation for management of commercial and real estate operations, the vice-presidency and general counsel of LTV Aerospace Corporation and service in Washington, D. C., as assistant to Lawrence F. O'Brien, special assistant to President Lyndon B. Johnson.

Mr. Humann is now executive vice-president of Hunt Oil Company and Officer of Hunt Investment Corporation for management of oil and gas operations, real estate, agriculture, and ranching interests.

His wife is the former Beatrice Read, of Dallas.

Agri-business, Manufacturing, and Other Industries

by WALTER J. HUMANN

Shortly before his death, the old man in an Aesop fable called his sons to his bedside. He told them that somewhere on the farm land he was leaving them was a vast treasure. No sooner was the father in his grave than his sons began spading and respading every foot of soil. But they found nothing. In their desperation they planted seeds in the tilled ground. To their later surprise they had the most bountiful crop ever produced in the area, and at harvesttime they made a rich profit. They finally realized that the treasure their father left them was in the richness of the soil itself and in the fruits of their individual and collective labors.

This story is not unlike the story of Dallas. Men and women, like the mythical sons, were attracted to Dallas by the hope of great fortune. Having come, they found the true wealth of the area in the richness of the land and in the character, ingenuity, and hard work of people who lived and labored here. These two factors, along with others, were the foundation for Dallas' ultimate prominence as a major agricultural and industrial center in this country.

DALLAS AGRICULTURE

Early History

In its native condition north-central Texas presented a panorama of gently rolling prairie covered with a spectrum of wild flowers and broken by clumps of mesquite, live oak, pecan, hickory, and cottonwood trees. The first European to see it was the Spaniard Luis de Moscoso in 1542. He was part of the ill-fated De Soto expedition and did not stay long. However, the subsequent development of herds of mustang

25

horses, a product of the Spanish barb, attracted Anglo-American horse hunters to the area in the late eighteenth century. Later, in 1819, David Long, whose brother helped to found the Republic of Texas, came to the muddy flats at the forks of the Trinity River to trade for horses with the Indians.

The men who founded the Republic of Texas in 1836 had a major asset—land. They established a liberal land policy which attracted Anglo-Americans, Mexican-Americans, and Europeans to the Republic. Large grants were offered to immigrant companies in order to develop buffer settlements against roving Indians of the plains.

With land as the magnet, enterprising promoters were attracted to the frontier. Such was the case in 1841 when John Neely Bryan settled near an easily fordable point on the Trinity River. John Neely Bryan cut a short, crooked cedar fork while building his cabin and used it as a suitable, if primitive, plowing implement for the following planting season. Thus he became the area's first Anglo-American farmer.

If Bryan was the first farmer, then his wife's relatives were Dallas' first ranchers. Her uncle, John B. May, came to the area in 1852 to raise horses, cattle, and sheep on a rich tract of land which is now the Oak Lawn area.

Ranching and Ranching By-products

The area around Dallas provided splendid pasture land for herds of horses, sheep, and beef and dairy cattle. In the great cattle drives of the late 1860s and the decade following, more than six million head of cattle moved out of Texas, many through the dusty streets of Dallas. As late as 1886 cattle were still being driven up Elm Street to Carter's Stockyard. Dallas also became known as the Southwest's largest market for buffalo hides.

It was legend that the notorious Belle Starr had a livery stable in Dallas that allegedly served as a clearinghouse for stolen horses and other such skulduggery.

Many of the pioneers who built Dallas expanded into commerce, finance, and manufacturing from an agricultural foundation. For example, Dallas claimed the saddle-and-harness-making title for the nation. It started in 1869 with Jesse D. Padgitt, a native of Tennessee, and G. H. Schoellkopf, a hard-working, enterprising German. Later pioneers in this industry included E. O. Tenison and Charles Steinmann. By the turn of the century, Dallas' leading manufacturers were turning out two hundred sets of harnesses a day at a then handsome sales volume of $5 million per year. Another example of an agricultural-based business was exhibited by Charles Adam Mangold. Of German descent, he introduced horse racing and harness racing to stimulate business for the State Fair. He also acquired a herd of Angora goats in the settlement of a debt. Mangold upgraded the herd and started production of some of the world's finest grades of mohair—unequaled among natural fibers for luster, durability, and strength. He also produced Mangold whiskey, very popular in Dallas.

Today, ranching around the immediate Dallas area has diminished. The elegant ranches that ring the area are only faint reminders of Dallas' former ranching prominence.

"King Cotton"—the Fiber Crop

If there was any one product that helped to make Dallas famous, it was cotton—that versatile, strong white fiber. After the Civil War, Dallas' farmers discovered that the surrounding blackland was ideal for growing cotton—profitably. In the fall of 1875 more than forty thousand bales of cotton were ginned near and compressed in Dallas. Lower Elm Street became a curb-side cotton market. By 1880 cotton traders annually bought and sold over fifty thousand bales. The Cotton Exchange was organized in 1907. The Gaston Building was erected at Commerce and Lamar to get the cotton traders off the streets; storage yards cleared the curbs. The volume of cotton business activity grew to such an extent that in 1925 the Cotton Exchange Building was built. It was one of the largest buildings in Dallas at the time and served as a symbol of Dallas' growing status as the center of cotton.

Cotton increased in importance to the point that following World War I, Dallas became the largest inland cotton market in the nation, if not the world. Foreign cotton merchants came from all over the world and settled here during the 1920s and 1930s. From Britain came many cotton men, among them Roger and Hugo Dixon and H. L. Edwards (who introduced golf to Dallas); from Germany came such men as Molsen, Lehmkuhl, and Humann; and from Japan Kamura, Shinohara, and others. These naturalized Americans settled here and added much to Dallas' cotton industry and culture.

Today cotton trading has declined in Dallas; but cotton merchants still risk their credit and fortunes on a grand scale. The Dallas Cotton Exchange continues to handle over $300 million annually. Cotton dealers buy and sell cotton world-wide, even though much of it is no longer shipped through Dallas.

Certainly, cotton was the agricultural product that propelled Dallas into world prominence as an agri-business center. With that base, many other industries were spawned.

Agricultural machinery and distribution grew into a major industry with Dallas serving a world-wide market. Cotton gin manufacture and repair became a leading Dallas industry. In the 1880s Swann Brothers opened a cotton gin repair shop at the intersection of Young Street and the Santa Fe tracks. In 1884 they began manufacturing complete gin units. A year later Robert Munger started building cotton gins that contained the most significant improvements since the invention by Eli Whitney. This early Dallasite's patented improvements and other cotton gin manufacturing giants like Murray Company (now part of Rockwell International) won Dallas world-wide prominence in cotton machinery.

Dairy Products

Dairy processing figured prominently in Dallas history. Beginning with a farming operation, J. William Smith, a shoemaker and cabinetmaker who migrated from Tennessee in 1854, settled on 250 acres fronting on what is now Webb's Chapel Road and Northwest Highway. Joined by his two sons, James and Charles, Smith raised dairy cattle and supplied milk and cream to the growing Dallas population. Later a small ice-cream establishment at Ross and Akard persuaded the Smiths to take over their financially troubled operation. Thus began the Smith Ice Cream Company, founded in 1898, using one ten-gallon "home-style" freezer. Smith Ice Cream Company grew and progressed with Dallas for sixty-eight years under the continuous ownership of J. William Smith's descendants until it was liquidated in 1966.

Today, Dallas dairy needs are supplied by national chains as well as local firms such as Cabell's, Metzgers, Schepps, Oak Farms, and Bluffview.

Farms and Food Crops

Besides meat and fiber crops, the Dallas area initially produced food crops as well as subsistence crops. Later, in the late 1800s large farms were developed that produced food crops of grain, corn, and certain other vegetables. These crops were grown on farms owned by some of Dallas' leading citizens of yesterday. Many of these farms were later to become part of Dallas' vast, developed real estate. Most of the land was owned by white farmers such as Caruth (at one time said to have owned more than thirty thousand acres of farm land in North Dallas). There were also successful black farmers, such as Keller (Keller Springs Road), Barton, Tarpley, Sowell, and McShann.

Early Dallas concern with agricultural science and research was exemplified by Colonel Henry Exall and the Texas Industrial Congress, an organization promoting cultural development and soil conservation throughout Texas. It was, in fact, a forerunner of the Texas Research Foundation at Renner, an agricultural experiment station now called the Texas A&M Research and Extension Center at Dallas. Colonel Exall assisted Texas farmers in organizing the Texas Industrial Congress, which had ten thousand members. Through the Texas Industrial Congress, Colonel Exall and other businessmen awarded $30,000 in gold as prizes to farmers who had done the best with what they had.

Agri-business Today

While farming and ranching in Dallas have given way to urban development, Dallas is privileged to have headquartered major publicly held firms in the food production and food retailing industries. These include:

OVERLEAF: Dallas from the west, at what was until recently a working farm similar to many that still surround the city. The Kenny Davis farm shown here has had to make way for the Dallas–Fort Worth Regional Airport.

Southland Corporation	Operates convenience grocery stores with sales over $1.4 billion.
Campbell Taggart	Bakery products.
Cullum Companies	Retail and wholesale food and drug outlets under the name Tom Thumb and Page.
Dr. Pepper Company	Soft drinks.
Neuhoff Brothers Packers	Meat packing.
Superior Foods	Produces convenience, refrigerated dough products.
Garland Foods	Meat producers. One of the most successful black businesses in the nation.
El Chico Corporation El Fenix Restaurants	Mexican-style food products. Two of the most successful chicano businesses.

In addition, there are many privately held firms that produce, process, and distribute meat, dairy, agricultural, and other food products to the area and the nation.

DALLAS BUSINESS AND INDUSTRY

First Steps for an Industrial Giant

While agri-business was developing and Dallas was becoming a commercial and transportation center, diversified manufacturing grew almost unobtrusively. Critics of Dallas claim that John Neely Bryan was the first "manufacturer"—producing the first whiskey to be sold. But the first true manufacturing operation was probably that of a displaced Frenchman named Maxime Guillot. Guillot's horse-drawn carriages had the reputation of being the finest carriages in the Southwest and were sold throughout the region. But Dallas had to wait until after the turn of the century to begin a major thrust into manufacturing with the introduction of a horseless carriage named after Henry Ford.

Dallas was successful in attracting wholesale and retail trade during the 1880s and 1890s. Many manufacturers and entrepreneurs followed the railroads, seeking to manufacture some of the goods closer to their Dallas markets. So it was that back on December 17, 1909, Henry Ford set up a two-man sales and service center for his then six-year-old company. It was on Commerce across from today's Statler Hilton Hotel. The work force quickly expanded to fifteen during the first year, and by 1913, assembly of Ford cars began at the site.

OPPOSITE: The Farmer's Market on the southern edge of downtown Dallas.

In the early days of the automobile, literally hundreds of companies manufactured cars, some in Dallas County. Scores of auto names flashed into bright, if temporary, prominence. As was to be the case so many times, Dallas attracted the successful company—Ford. By 1914 Ford had to build a bigger assembly plant, this time at Canton and Williams, which was renamed Henry Street. In its first year it produced 5,504 cars.

Eleven years later Ford completed a larger assembly plant on East Grand with a capacity of 350 cars and trucks per day. During World War II that Ford plant produced more than 100,000 military trucks and jeeps. In April 1947 the one-millionth Ford car "Built in Texas by Texans" (the long-time Dallas plant slogan) rolled off the assembly line. That was only thirty-eight years after the first Ford car was sold in Texas and thirty-four years after the first Ford was assembled in the old Commerce Street plant. The second million cars were produced in only ten more years, and the three-millionth Ford rolled out in January 1968.

Wholesale distribution of parts continues to be a major industry in the Metroplex for Ford, General Motors, and other transportation and agricultural and heavy equipment manufacturers.

As has happened so many times in the city's history, either an already established industry brought extraordinary men or extraordinary men brought industry.

As a result, shortly after 1872 the city began to experience phenomenal growth. Business people who had followed the railroads from one temporary Texas terminal to another now came to settle permanently where the railroads finally crossed. By 1890 Dallas had attracted the major lines of business and industry that were to support its economic growth for the next fifty years. Manufacturing increased slowly but steadily in Dallas, with minor setbacks—and a few major ones in depression years such as 1873, 1884, 1893, 1904, and 1907 (depressions were called panics then). The entire nation adjusted quickly in those days of plentiful opportunity for investors and enterprisers, but Dallas adjusted more rapidly than many other sections. Jobs in manufacturing totaled about 4,900 for 1904, but by 1909 they had jumped to seven thousand despite two "panics."

Industrial employment in nonmanufacturing jobs continued apace. Jobs in manufacturing enjoyed another steep rise from 1920 through 1929 in Dallas, despite sharp national economic setbacks in 1920 and 1929. The Great Depression caught up with Dallas by 1931, but while most of the nation struggled through massive unemployment in 1932 through 1935 and again in 1938 and 1939, Dallas was pulling out of the slump with sharp increases in manufacturing jobs from 1934 through 1938. An even sharper climb followed, as the United States became the "arsenal of democracy" and then began rearming for World War II.

Black Gold Takes Over from King Cotton

Dallas managed somehow, despite being one of the few of Texas' 254 counties with neither petroleum nor natural gas deposits, to build on the same innovative attitude of its cotton trading empire to create a new empire based on oil.

For six thousand years of written history, and for untold centuries prior to that, petroleum at best served humanity in severely limited ways. Mostly petroleum constituted a nuisance. Where it seeped to the surface it ruined crop land and water. Finding oil when digging for water proved a disaster to well digger and landowner alike before enterprising people created a use and a market for the viscous, stinky mess, turning it into black liquid gold.

As late as 1894, officials of the city of Corsicana considered the discovery of oil there to be a near-disaster, and it almost bankrupted the drilling company before it could close off the oil flow and bring in a much-needed deep artesian water supply for that growing city. Later a more farsighted group actually drilled for oil two hundred feet south of the artesian well. They hit, and late in 1895 they shipped out of Corsicana the first tank car of oil ever to leave Texas. Spindletop, near Beaumont, with the first use of the rotary drilling technique, in 1901 really brought oil fever to the world. Sour Lake, Electra, Burkburnett, Ranger, and other fields followed. By the 1920s, oil strikes included those at Laredo, Luling, Big Lake, Yates, Winkler, and Van.

It was only after the big East Texas Field was brought in by C. M. "Dad" Joiner and bought out and developed by H. L. Hunt in 1930 that Dallas got into the boom.

It was Dallas enterprise that built Dallas into a greater oil capital than Tulsa, long the most noted oil center. Oil, just like so many other endeavors, expanded within diversified commercial and industrial Dallas. Dallas had so many things going for it, and so many more on the horizon, that even black gold could not dominate the image of the city.

Production of oil required many essentials other than the oil well itself. Dallas, with no oil of its own, capitalized on those essentials. Financing, legal matters, geological science, transportation, oil well equipment, and other machinery manufacture and distribution all were "naturals" for the enterprising, creative men of Dallas.

Many oil and gas related industries are located in Dallas today, including the following publicly held companies:

Halliburton Company
American Petrofina, Inc.
Atlantic Richfield and many other majors
Lone Star Gas Company
Trinity Industries, Inc.
Dallas Power and Light Company
Southern Union Gas Company

SEDCO, Incorporated
Texas Oil and Gas Corporation
Earth Resources Company
General American Oil Company of Texas
Holly Corporation
Core Laboratories
Dorchester Gas Corporation
Sabine Royalty
Aztec Oil and Gas Company
Delhi International Oil Corporation
Hanover Planning Company
Triton Oil and Gas Corporation
University Resources
Maynard Oil Company
Lear Petroleum Corporation
Summit Energy, Inc.
Baruch-Foster Corporation
May Petroleum, Inc.
Oklahoma Oil
Planet Oil and Minerals

In addition, there are numerous privately held companies centered in Dallas such as Hunt Oil Company.

World War II Launches the Aerospace Age in Dallas

World War II generated new industries in Dallas and fostered dramatic growth in many established industries. Manufacturing employment in Dallas hit a high of 75,600 employees at the apex of World War II production in 1944. Such is the Dallas foresight and spirit of progress that the citizenry set to work, even as the supreme effort of production for war defense was winding down, to create goods and services to meet civilian market demands. On August 22, 1945—just two weeks after Japan's surrender—the first postwar Ford passenger car rolled out at the Dallas plant. By 1953, manufacturing employment had surpassed the top of 1944. The Dallas market area added an average of seven thousand manufacturing jobs per year from 1960 to 1970. In 1973 an increase of 10,800 manufacturing jobs exceeded the growth of any three other cities in the Southwest combined. Part of this growth during and after World War II was attributable to the aircraft manufacturing industry and other businesses servicing the military.

The aircraft industry in Dallas actually started with the building of a pilot training center here named after Lieutenant Moss Lee Love of the U. S. Army Air Corps. Airmen from throughout the United States came to train at Love Field. After World War I, activity subsided until the storm clouds of World War II gathered in Europe in 1939. Prior to American entry into the war, officials of North

American Aviation, Inc., in Inglewood, California, began construction of a major plant in the southwest part of Dallas County. It was completed in the summer before the Japanese attack on Pearl Harbor. The primary reasons for locating the plant in Dallas were (1) to disperse key industry inland in the event of a surprise attack, (2) to spread the economic base of rearmament across the country, (3) to tap the highly productive, trainable labor market in Dallas, and (4) to utilize adjacent Hensley Naval Air Field as a training base.

Chief source of pride to the Texans who worked in the plant was the famous P-51 Mustang, rated by most pilots as one of the best fighter planes of World War II and credited with winning the battle for air supremacy over Europe. The executives of North American Aviation found Texans highly motivated by a powerful sense of patriotism to continually improve productivity and production quality. Consequently, the Dallas plant of NAA earned one of the top productivity ratings (lowest cost per pound of air frame manufactured) of any plant in the country.

Immediately after World War II, the North American Aviation plant was closed. But not for long. An enterprising factory superintendent from Scotland, Robert McCullough, leased one of the abandoned buildings to start Texas Engineering and Manufacturing Company (TEMCO). TEMCO, initially employing one hundred to two hundred, made soft-drink dispensing machines, a wide variety of other consumer-related products, and eventually entered into the aircraft market.

Beginning in the fall of 1948, Chance Vought Aircraft of Stratford, Connecticut, moved its entire plant to the west side of the abandoned North American plant. The Dallas Chamber of Commerce had proved extremely persuasive. Under the leadership of Andrew DeShong and others, Dallas business and civic officials made many trips to Connecticut to convince Chance Vought management of the logic of a move to Dallas. Approximately thirteen hundred families moved from Connecticut to Dallas and represented the largest industrial move of its kind. That base of trained employees, plus local hiring, provided the initial nucleus of the Chance Vought plant.

Chance Vought initially produced the F4U-5 Corsair, also rated as one of the great fighter planes of aviation history. Later it manufactured the F6U fighter, the twin-engine Cutlass, and the F8U supersonic fighter. In recent years it designed and manufactured the light attack aircraft, the A7 Corsair II. By this time, Chance Vought and TEMCO had become part of the LTV Corporation, the largest Dallas-based corporation and one of the larger diversified companies in American business. This giant multi-industry company, with a sales volume of over $4 billion in steel, meat, and aerospace, had as its historical footing two Dallas-based aircraft entities.

As a result of the North American and later the Chance Vought moves, real estate and retail businesses were stimulated and satellite businesses were developed. These included small machine shops, processing and plating shops, tool and die makers, structural steel and sheet metal fabricators, welding and light manufacturing operations, technical consultants, computer operations, and a large number of

suppliers of goods and services. Numerous warehouses stockpile mountains of merchandise and materials for distribution throughout the region not only for aerospace industry but for other fields as well.

Today, the Dallas–Fort Worth Metroplex ranks among the five largest aerospace centers in the United States. Dallas area firms design and manufacture civilian and military aircraft and a wide variety of space and missile hardware and software.

Rocketing Ahead with Space-Age Diversification

New horizons stretched ahead after World War II, and Dallas businessmen, as always, forged ahead in creating new, further-diversified industrial and professional opportunities for residents and newcomers alike. Computer and electronics technology could be considered a natural companion for growth alongside the area's aerospace industry, but this growth did not come automatically.

Dallas-based companies shared in developing missile and space program concepts and hardware. Rocket, missile, and computer technology and the necessity for miniaturization of components helped to generate in Dallas new companies specializing in electronic and space-related research, engineering, and production. This expertise led to further diversification of Dallas industry as government-financed production began to give way to commercial development for private and foreign sale and use. While some companies failed and faded, others grew into thriving, specialized enterprises; some became diversified giants.

Texas Instruments, which ranked among the top half-dozen corporations in Texas and 126th nationwide in 1974 sales, grew from a tiny, suburban Dallas company of World War II days into a world-wide enterprise. TI plunged into the transistor business in 1952 along with twenty other companies which had obtained manufacturing licenses from Western Electric's Bell Telephone Laboratories. The small Dallas company had only the basic design for the tiny component that was about to revolutionize the electronics industry. TI discovered the technique of producing the high yields needed to make solid-state electronic equipment competitive economically with similar vacuum-tube equipment.

In 1954 TI produced the first commercial silicon transistors. By 1958 TI researchers had brought further dramatic changes in the industry. TI faced massive competition from Japanese and other foreign manufacturers from time to time during the 1960s and early 1970s, but ingenuity and hard work brought the company back into top leadership each time. Sales in 1974 exceeded $1.5 billion. Employment runs at 45,000 in thirty-six plants located in sixteen different nations.

By 1975 more than three hundred companies involved in one or more aspects of the computer and electronics fields gave Dallas extensive activity all across the spectrum of this complex industry, from manufacturing to sales and service. More than one hundred electrical and electronics manufacturing companies based in the Metroplex are doing business internationally.

OPPOSITE: The Trinity Industrial District, principally a distribution and wholesaling center extending almost to Irving between the Trinity River and Stemmons Freeway. The area also contains research facilities, small manufacturers, and other businesses.

Metroplex companies produce electronic calculators, digital clocks and watches, communications equipment, optical character recognition products, controls and indicators, microwave products and systems, radio, TV, and stereo components, burglar alarms, and specialized automotive components. The semiconductor division of Varo, Inc., for example, produces most of the high-voltage rectifiers used by major TV manufacturers.

Dallas now earns new stature for innovative capability, partly because of extensive research facilities. More than 1,850 scientists and engineers, along with 1,500 technical personnel, work in full-time research, not counting that performed in colleges and universities. Corporate research budgets total more than $380 million. The principal research areas are petroleum exploration and production, blood diseases, speech and hearing, biological fluids, floods, agricultural products, electronics, optics, aerospace, radiation, ecology, and communications.

Still More Diversity

Dallas ranks third in the nation in production of motion pictures and TV commercials. This includes feature pictures, industrial films, educational films, and video tapes. Dallas ranks fifth in the nation as a center for distribution of motion pictures to commercial movie houses.

Printing and advertising enterprises in Dallas lead the entire South and Southwest in this category of industry. At the beginning of 1975 more than three hundred printing and publishing firms employed more than 11,500 workers. Two major metropolitan newspapers, the Dallas *Times Herald* and the Dallas *Morning News,* provide competing print journalism for Dallas, a rare advantage that many much larger cities no longer enjoy. Dozens of newspapers for suburban communities and for churches, trade associations, civic clubs, and other private associations, both local and regional, are published by Dallas presses. Taylor Publishing Company is one of the world's leading printers of yearbooks for organizations and educational institutions. Ten prominent petroleum-oriented publications are printed here.

A major advertising center in addition to television commercials, Dallas supports more than two hundred advertising agencies and more than one hundred commercial art studios, plus numerous other companies supplying and servicing both.

Apparel design and manufacturing with a fashion scope and output for the national and international market is now one of Dallas' leading industries, ranking second only to New York and Los Angeles. It grew out of a jobbing business begun by August Lorch in 1907, and this evolved into the manufacturing of original ruffled house dresses by 1929. Earlier, in 1918 the wholesale firm of Higginbotham, Bailey, Logan began making men's work clothing, and two years later they started their own label of women's dresses. Out of that company emerged the manufacturers Justin McCarty (a Higginbotham nephew), John Donovan, and Lester Lief.

In 1925 the Marcy Lee Manufacturing Company of Lief and Wadel came to Dallas from Tyler. Later in 1940 came Gordon Edwards and his slacks for women. Since then the picture has become a huge industrial mural with company names such as Bernard Gold's Nardis, Herman Marcus, Page Boy, Robert R. Michlin, Howard B. Wolf, Jerrell, Donovan-Galvani, Malouf, Mr. Fine, Haggar, and Stockton of Dallas. The results are thousands of workers, millions of dollars, and the recognition and reputation of a great American fashion center.

So too in millinery is a Dallas industrial story. It began in the Gay Nineties when L. O. Daniel Millinery Company was founded. Then just after the turn of the century came Baron Brothers and Porter Company, and after World War I the names of Goldstein, Dallas Hat Manufacturing Company, Mancell-Wilson, R. B. Smith, Davis Company, Mittenthal, Rosenfield, and Rosen were established. Later after another world war the styling of Asbury Company, Jan Leslie, and others led another growth period into the size of the present market.

Along with the futuristic, the glamorous, and the exotic, mundane production and distribution always remain vital to the everyday life of a community and its citizens. Dallas-area development and production of such goods and services change with the times. If pleasure boat and mobile home building begin to fade in the Metroplex, recreation vehicles, travel trailers, and campers take up the slack. When fuel shortages curtail manufacture and distribution of such items, other markets for different products are sought and located, such as the cosmetic industry. If rising Dallas wage rates cause some apparel manufacturing to shift to smaller towns or to other regions of the nation, other products and services are developed, so that jobs and income continue to grow in Dallas.

Construction activity, both commercial and residential, averaged more than a billion dollars annually within the Metroplex for the past five years. Dallas contractors also win construction contracts nationwide and world-wide.

FACTORS CONTRIBUTING TO DALLAS PROMINENCE

As a California industrial executive put it when this area began its modern industrial expansion: "What these rural-bred workers don't know about technical skills they make up in willingness to learn, in industriousness, and in eagerness to get the job done right."

Where many major towns or cities have started with greater promise or enjoyed periods of spectacular growth, too often the promise or the boom resulted from the efforts of one man or one single economic factor. After Bryan started it all, Dallas never lacked for diversified, aggressive leadership. Some cities depend upon one man or one family to accomplish everything necessary for the progress of their community. No matter how conscientious and hard-working any one leader may be, he cannot do as well as a dozen leaders working, both together and in competition, to improve their city.

Dallas always seems to have dozens of men and women working together to accomplish whatever business needs doing. When it comes to improving the economic opportunities of Dallas and its citizens, business rivals usually co-operate for the benefit of all.

Dallas scored a major coup in the 1930s which illustrates how Dallas leadership has banded together. As Texans prepared to observe the centennial of their Declaration of Independence of March 2, 1836, almost every city, institution, and organization began making plans years in advance for special events and activities. One city would be designated as the site for the official state-wide centennial observance, with a commission appointed to select the most suitable centennial celebration site. Other Texas cities possessed great advantages in the competition,

but Dallas countered with farsighted, forearmed, and well-organized campaigners, led by R. L. Thornton and assisted by other Dallas businessmen such as Fred F. Florence, Harry A. Olmsted, Arthur L. Kramer, and A. Maceo Smith. They raised $3.5 million and enough rumpus in the right places to beat out all the others, who probably really had more right to the official designation than Dallas. But Dallas won it.

It is apparent to many why Dallas has maintained its position of industrial leadership in the Southwest for more than thirty years. One reason is the favorable attitude of the people. For a variety of reasons, employees are generally highly productive and better motivated. Second, Dallas' city administration has a good reputation nationwide. Third, Dallas has a stable business, labor, and educational environment which business must have in order to progress and expand. Fourth, Dallas has a varied population. The infusion of a large number of people from other parts of the United States has made Dallas a more diverse, stronger city. Fifth, Dallas has a balanced economy and a supportive banking and business community. Finally, the climate is ideal for attracting employees and for conducting business.

From the beginning Dallas established, first, a cotton and oil center, then a regional pre-eminence as a diversified commercial and industrial center, and then built a world-wide reputation in electronics, computers, and aerospace as well as other fields. Unlike so many major cities, Dallas never depended upon one or two dominant industries for its growth and progress. Diversified industry and commerce may not endow a city with a name and economic base—as steel did for Pittsburgh or oil for Tulsa or movies for Hollywood—but Dallas profited mightily through the years by being able to adapt to changing times and changing demands from the world's market places.

Another contributing factor is that the business community has generally been well organized. The Dallas Chamber of Commerce (which began as the Board of Trade in 1874 and later incorporated in 1908) has helped in Dallas' growth and development. Strong area Chambers of Commerce, the Dallas Mexican Chamber, and the Dallas Black Chamber of Commerce (which is celebrating its fiftieth year in 1976) have added to the dynamics of Dallas business and industry.

The labor force for metropolitan Dallas now totals about 900,000 persons, an estimated 6.5 per cent of whom hold multiple jobs. For the Metroplex, the labor force totals 1.2 million.

More than one thousand businesses based in the Metroplex number among the million-dollar corporations in the United States, including seven of the Fortune 500 largest publicly held companies.

Major publicly held companies located in Dallas are listed below by category:

ADVERTISING/MARKETING

Tracy-Locke Company, Inc.
Ammest Group, Inc.

AUTOMOTIVE

General Automotive Parts Corporation
K-B Industries, Inc.
Speed Equipment Worlds of America, Inc.

COMPUTER

Electronic Data Systems Corporation
Wyly Corporation
Recognition Equipment, Inc.
Computer Dimensions, Inc.
Carterfone Communications Corporation
Medical Computer Systems, Inc.
General Computer Systems, Inc.
National Data Communications, Inc.
ACS Investors, Inc.
Corporation S
Worldcom, Inc.
Britco, Inc.

CONSTRUCTION MATERIALS/CONTRACTING

Redman Industries
Gifford-Hill and Company, Inc.
Texas Industries, Inc.
Sam P. Wallace Company, Inc.
Slaughter Brothers, Inc.
OKC Corporation
Lane Wood, Inc.
Republic Housing Corporation

DRUG INDUSTRY/LABORATORIES

Southwestern Drug Corporation
American Biomedical Corporation

ECOLOGICAL/POLLUTION CONTROL

Burgess Industries, Inc.
Peerless Manufacturing Company
Sonics International

ELECTRONICS

Texas Instruments
Collins Radio Company
E-Systems
Summers Electric Company
Altec Corporation
Curtis Mathes Corporation
Docutel Corporation
Whitehall Corporation
Hall-Mark Electronics
Communications Industries, Inc.
Multi-Amp Corporation
Staco, Inc.
Elfab Corporation
Tocom, Inc.
Hydro-Metals, Inc.

HEALTH/BEAUTY

Mary Kay Cosmetics

HOME/OFFICE FURNISHINGS

Giffen Industries, Inc.
Overhead Door Corporation
Delwood Furniture
SMC Industries, Inc.
Campbell Manufacturing Company, Inc.

CLEANING/LAUNDRY

United Coin Services, Inc.
ALD, Inc.

METALS/CHEMICALS/MINING

Commercial Metals Company
Tyler Corporation
RSR Corporation
Great National Corporation
Magnolia Chemicals Company, Inc.

MILLINERY AND FASHION

Miller Brothers Industries, Inc.
Howard B. Wolf
Sue Ann, Inc.
Nardis of Dallas
Herman Marcus, Inc.
Donovan-Galvani Industries
Byer-Rolnick Company

REAL ESTATE

Centex Corporation
Lomas and Nettleton Mortgage Investors
Justice Mortgage Investors
Henry S. Miller Realty Trust
Bekland Resources
Forum Companies
Cardinal Corporation

RECREATIONAL EQUIPMENT AND FACILITIES

Columbia General Corporation
Anderson Industries
T-Bar-M, Inc.

RESTAURANTS

Steak and Ale Restaurants of America, Inc.
Bonanza International, Inc.
El Chico Corporation
Dairy Queen Stores
Pizza Inn, Inc.

TRANSPORTATION

Braniff International
Frozen Food Express Industries, Inc.
Chemical Express Company
Southwest Airlines
Trans-National Leasing

DIVERSIFIED

The LTV Corporation
Dresser Industries, Inc.
Zale Corporation
Michigan General Corporation
Pioneer Texas Corporation
Tem Tex Industries
Weil-McLain Company, Inc.
Coit International, Inc.
Chilton Corporation
Meisel Photocrom Corporation
The Riverside Press, Inc.
Olympus Service Corporation
Cimarron Corporation

CHALLENGES AND OPPORTUNITIES

As problems arise and grow from situations beyond the control of local, and even national, policies and efforts, Dallas will face greater challenges. Dallas has overcome major problems before. The destruction and bankruptcy of southern life, commerce, business, and institutions by the Civil War were taken in stride by Dallas citizens. The Great Depression failed to slow down for long the march of Dallas into greater accomplishments. When doom-criers forecast that the greatest depression ever was certain to descend on America after World War II, Dallas as a whole ignored the timidity and despair of the fainthearted. Dallas forged ahead on all fronts to lead the way to unprecedented growth and progress. Not only in quantity but in quality, Dallas living improved beyond the dreams of average citizens who grew up in the 1920s, '30s, and '40s.

Success and affluence can mislead those who come after the main struggles are

won. Even the leaders of progress can become complacent when major efforts succeed. Creators of Dallas agricultural, industrial, and commercial might are people who can look ahead and change with the times, not for the sake of change, but to preserve and improve the heritage passed on to them. People moving ahead need not look around for scapegoats. Busy people co-operate for the benefit of all. Communities that rest on their laurels or try to preserve failing institutions must succumb as the world passes them by. Progressive economies face problems that actually are challenges and opportunities.

DALLAS FOLKS

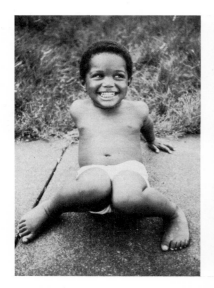

60

The governments of France, Austria, Italy, Denmark, England, and Belgium have all added their awards of honor in addition to the many bestowed by his own city, state, and country on Stanley Marcus for his expertise in the art of merchandising.

Born in Dallas in 1905, son of the cofounder of Neiman-Marcus, he received his academic degree at Harvard University. Mr. Marcus is chairman of the Executive Committee of Neiman-Marcus and corporate executive vice-president of Carter Hawley Hale Stores, Inc. In 1932 he married Mary Cantrell. His official and personal involvements on the business and cultural levels are manifold. He has been published in most of the major magazines and trade journals and is author of the book *Minding the Store* (Boston: Little, Brown, 1974).

Mercantile Life

by STANLEY MARCUS

The Houston and Texas Central railway brought its first train into Dallas on July 16, 1872, and in the words of A. C. Greene, "Nothing would ever be quite the same."

The H&TC was followed the next year by the Texas and Pacific, and soon thereafter by the Dallas and Wichita, the Texas Trunk, and other lines. Rail transportation brought along wholesalers and distributors of everything from dry goods and groceries to commission merchants, bankers, contractors, builders, retailers, and lumberyards. Thus, sixteen years after Dallas had been incorporated as a town and thirty years after the actual settlement of Dallas County, civilization rode in on the steel tracks of the railroads, and a mercantile life was born.

A pioneer society was faced with pressing problems for survival: defense against marauding Indians, planting and harvesting crops, the establishment of property lines, and involvement in the Civil War. With peace, wrote John H. Cochran in his book *Dallas County*, "Dallas gained and retained a large number of most useful and desirable citizens. These were ex-Confederates and ex-Confederate soldiers, who came from the border states where it was unpleasant for these former soldiers to live. They came to Dallas County not only seeking more congenial associates and protection from former enemies, but a place where they could restore and regain their lost fortunes."

Prior to the new era created by the junction of the H&TC and T&P railways, the little town called Dallas had been served by a few pioneer stores. J. W. Smith and James Patterson are credited with the first complete store, boasting a stock valued at seven hundred dollars, which "required two wagons to haul it from Shreveport, the trip taking forty days." It opened in 1846, as did the first saloon operated by one Adam Haught. Later in the same year competition began with the establishment of

With his brothers Philip, Isaac, Lehman, and Sam, Alex Sanger directed a mercantile empire that became nationally famous. The department store opened in Dallas in July 1872, though the German-born brothers had opened Sanger stores much earlier along the H&TC railroad route. In Dallas, Alex Sanger identified himself with every civic interest until the name became synonymous with the city. In 1879 he married Fannie Fechenbach, of Cincinnati. He died in 1925. COURTESY OF FRANCES MOSSIKER.

The founder of the oldest retail clothing store in Dallas, a twenty-five-foot-front shop opened on February 1, 1872, Emanuel Meyer Kahn was an Alsatian boy orphaned at fourteen who came to America on a packet boat that landed at Savannah, Georgia. His goal was to go west, and to him that meant Texas. He came to Dallas before the railroad when the stagecoach still ran to El Paso and ox-drawn wagons came in daily from the western frontier with buffalo hides and dried buffalo tongues to trade for supplies. Young Mr. Kahn grew into maturity and success with the town that he felt in his bones would be a city. Resisting personal publicity, he worked behind the scenes for local charities, the public library, the State Fair Association, Temple Emanu-El, and as a director of the American Exchange National Bank. The E. M. Kahn Company has continued to be a Dallas institution in downtown and suburban locations. Mr. Kahn was married to Lillie Hurst, of Jackson, Mississippi. He died in 1923. COURTESY OF E. M. KAHN & CO.

Simon Linz, born in St. Louis in 1862, came to Texas in 1878 to join his watchmaker brother, Joseph, who had opened a small jewelry store in Denison in 1877. Their other brothers, Albert and Ben, also joined them as they moved to Sherman in 1879 and then to Dallas in 1891. After several years in other buildings, Jos. Linz and Bro. opened their own seven-story "skyscraper" on Main Street during the gala State Fair of Texas in 1899. A thirty-third-degree Mason, Simon Linz created the annual civic award to the citizen whose leadership is of most benefit to the city, a selection made by committee from public nominations. It was first won by Elmer Scott in 1924. Mr. Linz married Beccie Epstein. of St. Louis, in 1889. He died in 1935. BROWNE & BROWNE.

a second general merchandise store by Charles Durgan and a man named Stanley. The town boasted a population of 430 in 1858, which encouraged a third retailer, Alex Simon, to open a general store which advertised "cheap prices for dry goods, groceries, hardware, ready-made clothing, paints and oils." Perhaps his was the forerunner of the modern-day discount store.

The progress of the railroads was watched very carefully by a group of retailers and pack peddlers known as "terminus merchants," who followed behind the railway construction crews. The railroad routes were predetermined, of course, but sudden changes were often made, for the railroads were susceptible to attractive offers from various communities which often bid competitively for railroad service. Consequently, it came as somewhat of a surprise that Dallas was going to become a junction point for the two lines, but the merchants moved hurriedly from Corsicana and in one day purchased seventy lots on Elm Street for business locations.

In 1872 the Sanger brothers, immigrants from Germany, built a store thirty by seventy feet on Main Street, opposite the courthouse, in which they sold everything from plows to dress goods and from notions to groceries. Shortly after opening their retail enterprise, they added a wholesale division and sent salesmen out on the road in spring wagons with spare mules hitched behind to call on customers in the adjoining counties. E. M. Kahn opened a wholesale and retail business a few months prior to Sanger's, and, in the same year, the firm of A. and E. Mittenthal established themselves as wholesale and retail dry goods merchants.

By 1875 shoppers who may have driven to Dallas in their buggies from nearby communities like Lancaster and Farmers Branch might have visited Sanger's and Kahn's for clothing, E. A. Worden for guns and sporting goods, E. Bauman for millinery and cloaks, F. Austen for jewelry and watches, and W. J. Shaw for books and stationery. They would have had to wait another year until they could purchase a piano or organ from C. H. Edwards. However, they could have refilled their larders at Menczer and Company, which specialized at that early date in Dallas' history in "imported and domestic groceries, fine wines and liquors, tobacco and cigars."

The Dallas City Directory for 1873, the year after the railroad entered Dallas, listed twenty-nine dry goods stores, ten druggists, eleven tobacconists, eleven shoe and boot makers, thirty-eight grocers, and one merchant tailor, R. A. Chambers by name, who specialized in "Scotch, English, and American cassimeres" (more familiarly known today as cashmeres). In the directory for 1886–87, there were only twenty-six dry goods merchants, but all other categories of trade showed vast increases: twenty-four druggists, twenty-two tobacconists, twenty-seven shoe and boot makers, 105 grocers, nineteen clothing dealers, ten merchant tailors, and seventeen dressmakers. The population of the city had doubled in this period, but the number of new mercantile establishments had doubled and then some.

Overleaf: View of Main Street eastward in 1887 with office poles for eight hundred wires.

The railroads had brought goods into town cheaper and faster than previously; they also brought immigrants, many of whom liked what they saw and stayed. A pioneer community had a pent-up demand for both the necessities of life and the luxuries of civilization that the merchants, fulfilling their historical role, provided.

One or two stores may serve the convenience of a buying population, but the presence of a number of competing retailers creates a market place that attracts customers from great distances. Wider assortments in style and prices are offered; the customer who comes to town to buy a suit may also be a customer for jewelry, sporting goods, and other articles handled by specialists. The buyer feels confident that if he can't find what he is looking for in one store, he will find it in another, and he has the satisfaction of knowing that he can compare quality and values from one store to another. This is one of the explanations of the success of today's suburban shopping centers. They are markets.

In 1885 the Dallas *Morning News* was founded, providing the citizens with an authoritative news source and the retailers with an important advertising vehicle. Fashion played little or no importance in the advertising messages; for the most part they announced the arrival of new shipments or proclaimed superior values. Today's jaundiced readers will find in them the same overly enthusiastic claims that many current ads carry. Hyperbole in 1885 was no different from hyperbole in 1976.

Sanger Brothers very quickly became the leading store in Dallas and retained its position of pre-eminence for many years. It was commonly referred to as the "Marshall Field of the Southwest." No greater accolade could any store receive in the latter part of the nineteenth century. Sanger's remained supreme despite increasing competition from newcomers to the department store scene, and it retained its position until the mid-twenties.

At the corner of Elm and Murphy a new store was organized in 1887 by Fellman, Graubach, and Harris. A year later it changed its name to A. Harris and Company when Adolph Harris bought out the interests of his partners. In 1897 William and Henry Green established a popular-priced department store on Elm Street, later to be known as W. A. Green. In 1890 Leonard Volk founded a family shoe store which eventually became Volk Brothers when his brother George joined him the following year. In 1891 Joseph Linz came to Dallas from St. Louis to open what was to become the finest jewelry store in the state, Jos. Linz and Bro., and in 1899 he built a seven-story skyscraper, the first in Dallas, to house his establishment. Governor Robert Taylor of Tennessee was later to describe it as "the diamond stud on the shirt bosom of Texas." Subsequently the Federal Reserve Bank was built behind the Linz store, giving rise to the quip that Linz had more money behind it than any other store in America. Arthur A. Everts became its competitor.

In 1901 Edward Titche moved to Dallas from Louisiana and joined forces with young Max Goettinger, a native of Berlin, to form Titche-Goettinger, which they

OPPOSITE: An annual occasion for major city-wide festivities in Dallas is the Neiman-Marcus Fortnight, during which the department store, with the co-operation of other organizations, sponsors numerous important cultural events. Here, flags celebrating the Italian Fortnight flutter above Neiman's windows over the heads of passers-by on Ervay Street.

Medallion Center on the Northwest Highway at Abrams Road.

established quite daringly uptown in a building later to be known as the Wilson Building, a far stretch from the center of retail activities at Main Street and at Elm and Lamar where Sanger's, the reigning monarch, was entrenched. But with the new century, Sanger Brothers found themselves facing formidable competition for the first time.

Sam Dysterbach started a dry goods store in "Deep Ellum" in 1903 to cater to the blue-collar workers and the blacks. He also specialized in uniforms for the police, fire department, and domestic help. The Cokesbury bookstore, organized and owned by the Methodist Church, first opened in Dallas on Elm Street in 1899 and later moved to its own building at Commerce and Field in 1906. In 1937 it built a large handsome bookstore on Main Street opposite Titche's.

As the hub of a geographical wheel, Dallas was in a unique position to act as a goods and services distribution center to the North Texas region, to West Texas, and to Oklahoma on the north. Large merchants bought their goods in New York, but the smaller ones used the facilities of the jobbers in St. Louis and Chicago and Dallas. It was natural that the manufacturing and wholesaling of saddlery found a

Dallas fashion queen, Kim Dawson.

At the Dallas Market Center, the Apparel Mart contains more than one million square feet of space and is only part of a vast complex of markets for wholesalers' displays.

large and ready market. G. H. Schoellkopf and the firm of Padgitt Brothers became the leaders in that trade. In 1872 Huey and Philip had established themselves as wholesalers, manufacturers, and retailers of "hardware, iron, tinner's stocks, house furnishing goods, etc." Sanger Brothers was the largest dry goods wholesaler, traveling the entire territory. Butler Brothers, wholesalers from Illinois, entered Dallas in 1909, and the Harris-Lipsitz Company, dry goods jobbers, moved from Tyler to Dallas, selling out in 1914 to a newly formed wholesale firm called Higginbotham, Bailey, Logan.

Stores have always incubated their own competition, for partners fall out with one another; ambitious young department heads save for the day they can go into business for themselves; a wealthy customer decides to back his favorite salesperson. Emanuel Meyer Kahn, a native of Alsace, was a polite soft-spoken man who had his office on a dais in the middle of his store at Lamar and Elm, opposite Sanger's. Whenever he had a troublesome problem, he turned it over to his vigorous, tougher partner and brother-in-law, Gerard Dreyfuss, to handle. He and Dreyfuss had a falling out when their respective sons had a disagreement, and Dreyfuss walked out and started his own men's store in 1910 at the corner of Main and Murphy, across from the City National Bank, and a short block away from the Santa Fe railroad terminal. His son Sol was no great merchant, but a marvelous, lovable person whose personality compensated for his lack of merchandising prowess. Kahn's was destined to spawn several other men's stores, for the Hurst brothers and Gus Roos later left to start their own men's wear business.

Herbert Marcus, born in Kentucky, began his retail career at Sanger's and his sister, Carrie, at A. Harris and Company. They left Dallas for a few years to live in Atlanta, but they returned in 1907 to start their own specialty store along with Carrie's husband, Al Neiman. They were fully aware of the competitiveness of the Dallas retail scene and the great financial resources of Sanger's in particular, but they believed the time was ripe for a different kind of store specializing in women's

Jefferson Boulevard, the "main street" of Oak Cliff.

ready-to-wear of the finest quality, appealing to the more sophisticated and affluent group of customers who had developed in the North Texas region. The initial advertisement for the new store proclaimed "the opening of the New and Exclusive Shopping Place for Fashionable Women, devoted to the selling of Ready-to-Wear Apparel . . . . a store of Quality, a Specialty store—the only store in the City whose stocks are strictly confined to Ladies' Outer-Garments and Millinery, and presenting wider varieties and more exclusive lines than any other store in the South." It is reported that Sanger's scoffed at the pretentiousness of the new venture and forecast an early failure which would bring Herbert Marcus back to Sanger's for re-employment. The prophecy was not fulfilled and the new business proceeded to make a modest success from the outset, gnawing away at the carriage trade that Sanger's had heretofore monopolized.

Philip Sanger died in 1902, so the sole direction rested in the hands of his brother Alex. There were two sons of the founders in the business, Eli, son of Philip, and Elihu, Alex's son. Either because of a lack of natural ability or because of the failure of the fathers to train them adequately, these two young men did not contribute what they should have to the sustenance and growth of the Sanger tradition. The critical reversal in the Sanger fortunes came about in 1921, with the deflation following the boom at the end of World War I.

In the spring of that year, R. W. Higginbotham of the wholesale dry goods firm of Higginbotham, Bailey, Logan believed that prices were going to drop. With prudence he decided that he didn't want to own high-priced inventory nor did he want to have a lot of accounts receivable of country merchants on his books. So he took an unprecedented step, called all of his salesmen off the road, and announced that Higginbotham's was not going to sell for fall. Alex Sanger decided to capitalize on the situation and booked both the normal Sanger wholesale business and Higginbotham's share as well. The market did collapse in the fall of that year, and Sanger's wholesale department was stuck with an inventory of goods no longer worth the marked price and accounts that were not collectible. Sanger's suffered huge losses which led to the eventual closing of its wholesale division. Alex Sanger died in 1925; and his nephew, Clarence Linz, son of Joseph Linz, the founder of Jos. Linz and Bro., and husband of Philip Sanger's daughter, Lois, was named president of Sanger Brothers. After several years of trying to manage the business, he sold it to the Jones Company of Kansas City. This sale, incidentally, was the first disposal of an important Dallas mercantile establishment to "foreign" interests, a process that was to be often repeated in the years to come.

Chester Jones, head of the acquiring company, took one look at the ages of the Sanger inventory and the Sanger staff and concluded that both needed slashing. Over a weekend, Sanger's released some fifty long-time employees, including saleswomen, floorwalkers, seamstresses, and fitters. Neiman-Marcus made a bold move for a small business and employed every one of them. This proved to be a tremendous blunder for Jones and a great coup for Neiman-Marcus, for the community was incensed by the inhumanity of Jones's action in the peremptory firing of the employees, and hundreds of customers followed their favorite salespeople and fitters to Neiman-Marcus. If there was any one turning point in the history of the latter firm, this was it.

The Sanger business did not fare well under Jones's ownership, and it was sold in 1951 to Federated Department Stores which poured ample capital into it. In 1961 Sanger's bought A. Harris and Company from the grandsons of the founder, who had discovered other things in life which interested them more than playing store. Sanger-Harris, as the merged company was named, was relocated in a new store building at Pacific and Akard, and embarked on a massive suburban development program that restored Sanger's to a position of dominance in the moderate-price department store field.

A variety of factors was responsible for the sale of retail store properties: the spectre of inheritance taxes, the need for greater capitalization, a desire to cash in the chips, and the failure of a second generation to carry on with the merchandising insight of the founding merchants. Titche-Goettinger had been absorbed by the Allied Department Stores in 1928, Dreyfuss and Son by Woolf Brothers of Kansas City in 1928, W. A. Green by Sperry and Hutchinson in 1950, Gus Roos by Norman Alweis in 1951, Linz by Gordons of Houston in 1965; Neiman-Marcus merged with Broadway-Hale of California (now Carter Hawley Hale) in 1969, and Volks sold out to Colberts in 1970.

Following World War I, James K. Wilson opened an upstairs men's clothing store which he named Victory-Wilson, not in patriotic fervor but because his partner was named Victory. He changed the name to James K. Wilson in 1934.

In 1937 the Zale brothers moved the headquarters of their credit jewelry chain from Wichita Falls to Dallas. Over the years this chain has grown to be the largest of its kind in the world. It absorbed the Levine stores in 1966, Skillern's drug chain in 1965, and Cullum and Boren, the largest sporting goods store in Dallas, in 1969.

The Cullum brothers, Bob and Charles, took their father's wholesale grocery business and turned it into the Tom Thumb grocery chain, the largest Dallas-based food operation.

No chronicle of the retail life of Dallas would be complete without recognition of the part played by the big national chain department stores. Sears Roebuck entered Dallas in 1912 with the establishment of a large regional mail-order plant, to be supplemented by its first retail store in 1925. It, J. C. Penney, and, to a lesser extent, Montgomery Ward became the anchor stores in many of the numerous suburban shopping centers. The first shopping center in Dallas was the one built by Edgar Flippen and Hugh Prather in 1931, the Highland Park Shopping Village, as part of their residential development. It was several decades ahead of its time. Of the regional centers, Wynnewood erected in 1949, NorthPark in 1965, Town East in 1971, Valley View in 1973, and Red Bird in 1975 are the most important.

The traditional and most successful shopping center format is the single or multi-mall design with large department stores located at each end as magnets to draw customers back and forth past and into the doors of the small shops, some of which are locally owned and operated and others of which are part of national chains, designed and decorated to look like independent boutiques.

So great has been the effect of the shopping centers that the percentage of retail volume done in the central downtown business district declined from 26.2 per cent of the entire city's retail volume in 1948 to 11.9 per cent in 1972. With the exception of expansions to Neiman-Marcus in 1950 and 1964, Titche's expansion in 1954, Cokesbury's in 1937, and the new Sanger-Harris store, there has been no major new mercantile store building in the downtown area in forty years. The growth has all been in the suburbs, where not only the big stores have gone, but hundreds of small shops as well, many of which have been independent specialty stores, such as Lou Lattimore, Marie Leavell, Lester Melnick, and the Carriage Shop. Although the big fish tend to swallow the little fish, there are still opportunities for the little fish to continue to live and grow, and what's more, the little fish feed off the traffic that the big fish attract to the shopping centers.

The twentieth century has witnessed the rise and decline of the American city. The popularization of the automobile made it possible to live outside the city and still enjoy all of the benefits of the city—its cultural attractions and its numerous activities. With the movement of families to the suburbs, retailing followed and built outpost shops in the first strip shopping centers. When it was discovered that people actually liked and preferred shopping away from town, the first small shops were replaced by large stores, as large as or larger than their downtown headquarters. The threats and fears of school integration contributed to the process of decentralization, but it was already in progress long before the Supreme Court ruling, as families chose to live in the suburbs instead of in the blighted inner core of the city.

There is an old Chinese proverb that may be apropos to the future of Dallas: "To prophesy is extremely difficult—especially with respect to the future." Can downtown Dallas be revitalized as a center of retail activity? Can people be persuaded to live in close proximity to the business district? The answer to the second question will probably provide the answer to the first. The prospects for the revival of downtown are dim unless some dynamic new elements are introduced, such as the proposed city lake or subsidized housing. Gas rationing, of course, could be influential in encouraging urban residence. If any of these things come to pass, there would be a reason for people to return willingly to town; downtown malls and new street lights aren't enough.

The retailers of Dallas contributed greatly to the growth of the community, giving time and money to a variety of enterprises that would make Dallas grow and that would add to the quality of life for its citizens. Alex Sanger, Ed Titche, Herbert Marcus, Arthur Kramer (the lawyer son-in-law of Adolph Harris who directed the affairs of A. Harris for many years)—all beat the pavements to raise funds to underwrite worthy causes. Among the group there were a few real merchants who would have made it in any league: Philip Sanger, E. M. Kahn, Herbert Marcus, Max Goettinger. These were men who knew merchandise by feel and sight, who knew their customers personally, and who used their influence to guide their patrons' purchases wisely. They were operating single-store units, and they were able to appraise the size and quality of their stocks visually, to greet their customers by first names. The new era of retail distribution has brought multiple stores which can be operated efficiently only by the added services of the computer. The customer is now a market; the person is now a number.

Sanger's had set a standard for good quality; Titche's amplified it by bringing into the market better quality, particularly in the fields of millinery and furs, and

Neiman-Marcus topped them all by bringing the best of whatever existed from all parts of the world. Advertising showed changes with the entry of Neiman-Marcus, for fashion began to be commented on in the daily advertisements as well as exceptional value. Stores around the nation subscribed to the Dallas *Morning News* to see what Neiman's was promoting. With Neiman's success in selling fashion, the other stores started to make their own advertising reflect more fashion stories. The women of Dallas began to get a state-wide reputation, soon to be followed by national recognition, for being among the best dressed in the country. Women traveled from Houston, Tyler, West Texas, St. Louis, and New Orleans to take advantage of the superior shopping facilities Dallas offered. The Neiman-Marcus fashion shows at the Baker Hotel and later its spectacular night shows encouraged manufacturers to try out new fashions in Dallas because of the responsiveness of the Dallas audience. The Southwestern Apparel Manufacturers' Association staged important semiannual shows for their retail accounts which contributed to the reputation of Dallas as a fashion center.

What made Dallas more receptive to fashion and quality than other cities in the area? First, it was the second largest city in the state for many years. Second, its population enjoyed a higher average income than other neighboring cities. Third, and probably most important, its citizenship was more cosmopolitan. As the center for cotton marketing, there were a number of Europeans living in Dallas who must have influenced others by their own tastes. The junction of the railways at Dallas brought a host of traveling salesmen from the East, and their dress and manners probably wore off some of the natural provincialism of the inhabitants of this new city. There were few traditions emanating from a strictly southern heritage which had to be overcome.

Finally, the participants of the ill-fated Réunion Colony, established in 1854 on the west banks of the Trinity by a group of French, Belgian, and Swiss refugees, many of whom had been forced to leave Europe by the coup of Napoleon in 1851, undoubtedly made an important contribution to the early taste standards of Dallas. A. C. Greene, in his excellent history, *Dallas,* described them as a "curious mixture of artists, aristocrats, dabblers . . . [who] added something to Dallas that few frontier towns of any size were to have: intellectual and artistic awareness—curiosity and acceptance of the best things of the mind and the heart. . . . They not only gave Dallas a taste of music, dancing, painting and poetry . . . [but] because of La Réunion, Dallas had fine tailors, lithographers, dressmakers and milliners, weavers, watchmakers, jewelers, stonemasons, cooks and vintners."

Changing times require new solutions. Increased inheritance taxes have made it difficult to pass a privately owned business from one generation to another in the twentieth century; hence the tendency toward the "sellout" to national retail chains owned not by single families but by general public investors, whose sole interest lies in the rate of profits achieved.

Founders of retail enterprises were usually motivated both by profits and by a quality of idealism. They wanted to run a store in a particular way, to express their personal tastes and standards, to help build the community in the certain knowledge that they would eventually benefit by the growth of the city, even at the expense of immediate profit. They owned their businesses and they were willing to take leadership roles; they had no one other than a brother or partner to whom they had to be accountable.

The chain store is operated by an appointed professional manager, who is held accountable for profit accomplishments *only*. If he doesn't succeed in achieving the profit goals set by the home office, he will surely be replaced by another manager. This obviously has an effect on the character of the business and its relationship to the public. In many cases, the stores become more efficiently managed, but in the course of time they lose individuality and tend to look like one another, with floor racks overloaded with apparel and counters stocked so heavily that displays become invisible. The sharp rise in shoplifting can better be attributed to the retailers' overexposure of merchandise than to a change in moral standards.

Sanger's today makes more money than it ever did under the Sanger family management because it is infinitely larger in size and because it is extremely well managed in the best tradition of its profit-oriented parent, Federated Department Stores. Sears and Penney's are superbly operated formula stores that look like their sister stores in dozens of other cities. Titche's has suffered from frequent top management changes, deterioration of the neighborhood adjacent to its downtown location, and a difficult competitive situation in the suburban markets.

In the seven years that Neiman-Marcus has been merged, its local management has retained operating autonomy and has maintained its reputation as a highly sophisticated specialty store. After fifty years of close association with the company, it was time that this writer give way to younger merchants in the day-to-day conduct of the business. No one can foresee if the new team will run the business in the same manner as its predecessors, or if the law of economic determinism fueled by the necessity to achieve a high price earnings ratio, so essential for any publicly owned business, will force pressures that could change the character of Neiman's.

With Lord and Taylor and Brooks Brothers recently added to the list of important retailers in the city, Dallas has a good balance of fine department and specialty stores. The strength of the North Texas Metroplex lies in its fortunate geographical location—as the hub of a wheel whose spokes, reaching in all directions, make access by car and plane an easy matter. Dallas itself will never be as large as Houston, but the burgeoning Metroplex area should retain its position as one of the dominant retail centers of the country.

Dallas has earned the reputation of being a quality market; the Dallas public has always supported the best and has shown great taste in the clothes it buys. In fact, its taste in clothes has been better than in its homes or the food it eats. The taste of Dallas is on its back—not in its mouth.

Born in Boston, Massachusetts, in 1921, Raymond D. Nasher received his education at the Boston Public Latin School, Duke University (Phi Beta Kappa), Boston University, and Harvard University, where he has recently taught and lectured as Honorary Visiting Fellow. An honorary doctorate was conferred on him by Southern Methodist University.

From 1943 to 1946 he served as an officer in the U. S. Navy on land and sea duty, and in 1951 he came to Dallas. His wife is the former Patsy Rabinowitz, of Dallas.

As president of the Raymond D. Nasher Company his business activities are focused on real estate development and investment banking with accent on regional shopping centers (such as NorthPark in Dallas), housing, office buildings, and industrial parks.

Mr. Nasher is also chairman of the board of NorthPark National Bank and is director and/or trustee of a number of varied cultural organizations in the city. He has also served as U. S. delegate to the General Assembly of the United Nations and as a member of many national committees and commissions on urban study.

Real Estate Development

by RAYMOND D. NASHER

1843–1870

In the beginning there was the land.

It was free for the taking, a gift of one square mile from the Republic of Texas to any pioneer family. John Neely Bryan could not resist it.

Dallas was not the product of men who sought solitude at the westernmost reaches of America. A merchant lawyer from Tennessee, Bryan raised his hut on the Trinity with the expressed purpose of creating a town. He had done it in Arkansas by developing Van Buren. He would do it in Texas. The promoters of the Peters Colony, the Texas Emigration and Land Company, advertised in the United States for newcomers. But their maps of North Texas offered no "place," no city to suggest civility. Bryan, determined to promote his town, gave it a name, personally drew its plat, and soon had it on all Peters Colony maps being distributed. Only a bold promoter would attempt to assemble people and create a city when all around land was being given away. Bryan did so, and was successful, for other emigrants soon settled near his cabin on a small bluff above Preston's Road ford on the Trinity River.

Bryan's cabin stood where the Old Red Courthouse stands today, and the river ran about where the Triple Underpass is. Bryan was only the first of several eager entrepreneurs: to the north a former Texas Ranger, Tom Keenan, had established a larger settlement known as Farmers Branch (1843); a short time later came Cedar Springs, less than two miles north of the new Dallas; and a rival settlement, Hord's Ridge, became William Hord's beginning (in 1845) of what is currently Oak Cliff. Other pioneers such as Bryan's new father-in-law, John Beeman, were content to homestead. He settled on White Rock Creek to farm.

None of the streets on the separate plats bore any relationship to the rival communities. When in the future the City of Dallas encompassed all of these various neighborhoods, the streets would present some interesting veers and turns. As a matter of fact Bryan learned, shortly after surveying and platting his village, that he had platted land already granted by the Peters Colony, and part of his 640 acres overlapped a grant known as the Grigsby Survey. Ten years lapsed before he received a confirmed plat. Nevertheless, confusion was to reign, for in 1874 Grigsby's heirs claimed vast and valuable parts of downtown Dallas. At one point

The first building in Dallas, the John Neely Bryan cabin now stands in front of the Dallas County Records Building, less than a mile from its original site.

over three hundred related property suits were before the Supreme Court of Texas. Primarily because of the Grigsby Survey, streets ran at angles to each other and failed to intersect or have the same width of right of way.

Bryan persisted. He gave lots to young married couples, became postmaster, and lobbied successfully for the creation of Dallas County. Two years later in a close vote Dallas became the county seat. This title and role as a purveyor of law and order on the frontier was of paramount importance. Dallas was finally established. Yet within a couple of generations, Bryan and most of those who followed him to Dallas had sold their real estate and had lost themselves in the great American metropolitan experiment. Bryan later confessed that for all his efforts, he had never managed to make any money in his Texas real estate venture.

The promise of a "fresh start" in a brand-new state annexed to the Union in 1845 brought an influx of settlers from the Old South. By 1850, the U. S. Census showed more than 2,500 people in Dallas County—and there might have been more had not California's Gold Rush lured some families to a greater promise in the West. Bryan himself left his creation for two years to seek his fortune in the West.

In 1856, four years after the first suburb, the Caruth Addition, was developed by a storekeeper, the town was incorporated. Four years later except for the courthouse and another brick building, the entire town burned. This tragedy and the ensuing Civil War were a low point in Dallas' development. But by 1871 the postwar politicians, retailers, and gamblers had sufficiently revitalized the town for it to receive a city charter from the state.

1872–1900

The first thing that happened was the growth of Dallas' downtown area. This growth was created by the arrival of two railways and in turn sparked the development of a streetcar network. In thirty years, spurred by its transportation, the town's population grew from three thousand to forty-three thousand. Dallas' position as a railhead allowed it to prosper despite the 1873 Panic. First it was the buffalo hide capital, then in 1880, Dallas claimed to be the world's saddle and harness making center. Cotton was also fast becoming a major crop, and Dallas was its shipping port. It was then that Dallas established its reputation as a market center, a reputation it has never lost.

The city's residential patterns began to be affected by the unanticipated magnitude of its growth. The exclusive residential section to the south, near Browder Springs, the Cedars (1871), was thought to be well sited. Yet new housing, streets, and streetcar lines began to radiate north and eastward because of the southern barrier created by the river. Across the river the first major attempt to develop Oak Cliff came in 1886. T. L. Marsalis and a partner bought two thousand acres and

began the promotion of the costliest suburb in Texas history. Marsalis met disaster because his timing was wrong. His plan for total development was somewhat premature, and he also felt the financial stringencies of the Panic of 1893.

The railroads that had come to Dallas were a challenging concern. It was believed by many that the so-called terminal merchants would set up shop near the tracks, and as the tracks crossed a mile from Dallas, this course might lead to the decay of the old downtown section near the river. Instead, many of these merchants, with the Sangers prominently among them, moved immediately to the old town. (The Sanger, Linz, and Dreyfuss families later had homes in the Cedars, thereby preserving its character into the twentieth century.) This influx marked the beginning of some of Dallas' major industries—wholesaling, general merchandising, and retail sales.

By the turn of the century the downtown boasted three hundred saloons, numerous gambling halls, a public school, a new city hall, several hotels, and finally the Sanger Brothers famous new store. In 1891 the county erected the existing red sandstone courthouse, its fifth. A highly textured architectural form with a Romanesque revival style, it competed strongly with the handsome courthouses in many surrounding counties, all of which proclaimed law and order's arrival in the wilderness.

1900–1940

New housing developments moved north and east. The new planned suburb—Munger Place—by 1905 rapidly became the prestige area in East Dallas. This area could actually boast more paved streets than the city. Various speculators since the 1880s had built residential additions to Dallas, some of doubtful aesthetic value, a few of them soundly planned and beautiful. Fairmont Street and Maple Avenue were for years choice residential areas. All but a few relics of its heyday, when it was a quiet and prestigious tree-lined street, are gone now.

A milestone in development followed T. W. Armstrong's purchase in 1907 of a large North Dallas tract of land from Colonel Henry Exall. Armstrong had been an early partner of T. L. Marsalis in his Oak Cliff venture but withdrew in a dispute before the project's collapse. Colonel Exall had dammed Turtle Creek to form "Exall Lake," and McKinney Avenue's trolley service extended to the lake. It became a popular "resort" for summer outings. From this widely known place began the growth of Highland Park.

In a time when the terms "city planning" and "zoning" were not yet well defined in Dallas, Highland Park was designed by Wilbur Cooke as an exclusive residential area. Cooke, then also designing Beverly Hills, produced an intimate plan in which neighborhoods, parkways, and parks reinforced the area's natural topographic

features. The Armstrong sons-in-law, Hugh Prather and Edgar L. Flippen, would not sell a lot until the type and size of house to be built upon it had been approved. It was part of the contract that the property be used for a home for at least twenty-five years. For two decades not one single commercial enterprise was built on any of the 1,275 acres of Highland Park. In 1932 Highland Park Village was finally opened after careful planning and development. The back of the center was designated for service and its entrance faced a major road. The controlled traffic pattern that was established gave it the national distinction of being the experimental prototype of present-day shopping centers. During its municipal development, Highland Park built and maintained a district character as well as its own city government. Like its later neighbor, University Park, it has steadfastly refused to be absorbed into the fold of the mother city, Dallas, that surrounds the two island communities.

Elsewhere, the consequences of Dallas' unplanned and unmanaged growth, disconnected neighborhoods, misaligned streets, inadequate public utilities, and the absence of a park system began to be noticed. Civic groups gave Dallas its first city plan in 1910. Prepared by George Kessler, the plan proposed a civic center downtown, grand city entrances, and parkways connecting comprehensively planned parks. With the exception of Turtle Creek Parkway, only the more utilitarian proposals such as flood-control plans and street improvements were carried out. Yet these ideas occasionally surfaced in private development projects such as the 1928 Greenway Park Subdivision. David Williams, a local architect and early mentor of architect O'Neil Ford, designed it with broad commonly owned "greens" several years before a similar planning approach was highly publicized in Radburn, New Jersey.

With an increase of 250,000 people in these four decades, the city was primarily concerned with housing growth and expanding its limits. The automobile became less of a luxury during the 1920s and 1930s, and further stratified the population. The extensive urban federal road-building programs being planned in Washington had yet to take effect. While pockets of fine homes still could be found in almost any section of the city, the well-to-do areas generally were on Swiss Avenue and Munger in East Dallas, throughout the Park Cities, along Turtle Creek, in North Dallas, and by the 1930s, along the shores of White Rock Lake.

Dallas' role as host to the 1936 Texas Centennial should not be overlooked. The exposition gave the city its most significant civic buildings of the thirties.

1940–1975

The Roaring Twenties and the exposition years of the 1930s left Dallas with a quarter million people spread over forty-five square miles—a density never afterwards equaled. Since 1940 Dallas, like many other cities, has redesigned itself to accommodate automobile roadways initially spawned in state and national legislatures in the mid-1920s. Roads literally paved the way to newly annexed land rapidly being developed to house the postwar influx of veterans. New outlying commercial centers sprang up along the roadways to serve automobile-scaled neighborhoods. Although this growth began to loosen Dallas' previously tightly woven urban fabric, the downtown area continued to boom. Apparently unconcerned with the city's decreasing density, the Central Business District continued to expand by growing up instead of out. Each new building was planned to be a little taller than the last. In new office space, Dallas was, for a time, second only to New York City. In the number of home offices of insurance companies, Dallas became third behind New York and Hartford. The two largest banks in Texas were in Dallas. Dallas was a major financial center.

The downtown area changed dramatically. For twenty years the thirty-three-story Magnolia Building (1921), a tribute to the fledgling Texas oil industry, had been the tallest building. Beginning with the Mercantile National Bank in 1942, the banks took the lead in vertical building. After the war, the Republic National followed with a thirty-six-floor tower (1954) and the First National stacked up fifty stories in 1960. The First also built the last architectural "bank statement," a monumentally mirrored mass extending fifty-six stories called the First International Building (1974).

Major Dallas insurance companies paced the banks' early building programs with the Employer's Insurance and Rio Grande Life buildings (1948 and 1949 respectively). Insurance long has been large in Dallas, but the years between 1950 and 1965 saw the most outstanding growth. This industry's major civic contribution, the Southland Center (1958), put together a 600-room hotel, an office building, and beautifully landscaped grounds. It still stands as a major architectural and planning success.

Approaching Dallas across the prairies, these looming towers advertise the city's chief industries, banking and insurance. Most have elaborate night lighting systems to accentuate their significance. Just as New York's skyscrapers are often photographed from across the East River, the beauty of these towers is enhanced when contrasted with the Texas plains. Frank Lloyd Wright, a strong advocate of this principle, once demonstrated its power in Bartlesville, Oklahoma. In 1946 he planned a second and higher "prairie tower" for Dallas. This was to be an urban hotel with an all-glass façade. Construction was announced but prevented by the developer's death.

It was 1955 before a concerted community effort brought a new major hotel to the city, the Statler-Hilton. That sparked the Sheraton's interest in Dallas—and its subsequent inclusion in the Southland Center.

Hotel growth moved the city to implement shelved postwar plans for a Civic Center. The handsome one-million-square-foot Convention Center added in 1971 to the auditorium (1957) has now made Dallas one of the top four American cities for convention business. Adjacent to the Convention Center complex, architect I. M. Pei's new City Hall (to be completed in 1977) will provide Dallas with a civic center closely tied to the city heart, in keeping with its 1944 City Plan.

The same plan, prepared by Dallas planner Harlan Bartholomew, also recommended Kessler's early parkway proposals, cited the city's scenic Turtle Creek Boulevard success, and outlined others designed to ring the city. In anticipation of the postwar surge, it proposed organizing subdivisions into neighborhoods coordinating the development of parks with schools. But after the war growth came so fast that all resources were needed to provide basic services to developing areas with no money budgeted for amenities. And as new and improved roads pushed the city's borders into the country, downtown merchants began to review their positions.

For the twenty years prior to 1940 Dallas' density averaged about ten people per acre. Downtown retail businesses thrived, but with the expansion and improvement of the one-mile-square street grid network, the predominantly radial streetcar system no longer worked. Downtown was no longer "The Place," only another place. The vertical thrust of major institutions in the Central Business District was doing something else to the city's inner core. Downtown property became too expensive for traditional shops and many "Mom and Pop" stores to remain. Highly accessible intersections such as those of two major thoroughfares or a crossroad with a federal highway began to be developed as secondary shopping precincts. By the time the Central Expressway was completed in 1950 major centers throughout the city—Preston Center, Inwood, Wynnewood Village, Westmoreland, Pleasant Grove, and Parkdale—none of which bordered on Central, were underway or already finished. They were needed: the city's incorporated area grew from forty-five square miles in 1940 to 277 square miles in 1960. Its 1960 density of 3.8 people per acre reflected the new automobile-oriented suburban life-style and lots large enough for "a pool in the back." These shopping area names quickly became a fixed part of Dallas' geographical lexicon as a necessary guide to many similar-sounding subdivisions.

However internally oriented, few of these 1950s suburban centers had the character of their 1932 prototype, Highland Park Village. Parking requirements had increased. Many newer centers were fragmented and confusing, most included some street-oriented commercial strips, and few were well landscaped. Again, just as in the Central Business District, in its open suburban centers Dallas demonstrated a "city utilitarian" versus a "city beautiful" approach to its new growth.

In 1965 NorthPark Center opened and offered something new in shopping. It had enclosed malls and plazas, a unified design, and climate control, and it was the first of its kind in Dallas. NorthPark's hundreds of trees, cultural events, sculpture, and fountains are something that shoppers have now come to expect in regional centers across the nation. Subsequent centers such as Town East and Valley View, newer industrial districts, and office parks have incorporated many of these ideas and improve life in Dallas.

Retail stores were not alone in their decentralization. Company offices, medical facilities, and various manufacturing and employment centers no longer felt tied to downtown commitments. The Oak Cliff Savings and Loan Building (1954), the Meadows Building, and Exchange Park (1965), a combined office and retail complex, all reflected a growing demand for exclusive suburban office accommodations. More recently office towers, particularly those of financial institutions, have begun to appear on the fringes of older suburban shopping centers. With these mixed retail, office, and entertainment uses blending into established residential neighborhoods, some suburban shopping areas may now be termed true village centers. The creation of the Dallas Market Complex on Interstate 35 meant the exodus of another major Dallas enterprise, wholesaling, from the downtown to a highly specialized "place" of its own. In 1950 a new nine-story Merchandise Mart had been built downtown east of the new City Hall. Ten years later most of those wholesaling exhibitors moved to the new one-million-square-foot Trade Center, complete with a dramatic five-level landscaped interior court. This Market Complex, several miles from downtown, now includes six buildings comprising almost five million square feet of indoor area set on 135 acres of land in the 1,200-acre Trinity Industrial District, reclaimed from the river's flood plain in 1928. It's a good example of Dallas' penchant for deliberately creating new urban patterns.

The postwar housing boom was not short-lived. Like a reflection, the suburban towns of Arlington, Irving, Garland, Grand Prairie, Mesquite, and Richardson grew in ratio to Dallas' population. In the ten years before 1950, the Dallas population rose 47 per cent, and 56 per cent during the following ten years. Housing became scarce, jobs plentiful. Preston Hollow and many other incorporated areas were brought into the city as future home and industrial sites. Dallas' incorporated area increased 615 per cent in those twenty years. Single-family housing developments highlighted these two decades of growth in Dallas after World War II. Young men home from the war took brides, started families—and the "home of our own" was part of the dream. Favorable financial terms permitted by the GI Bill and Federal Housing Administration programs provided no down payments, with interest rates on mortgages between 4 and 5 per cent with terms of the loan spread over twenty years or even longer. There was a ready profit for developers and builders. Thousands of young couples starting families were eager customers for the single-family homes that went into virtual mass production. Spreading over wider and wider areas were row after row of unimaginative but popular-priced housing. Land prices in unlikely places far from the central city went from a few hundred dollars per acre to thousands and tens of thousands dollars per acre. And single-family housing followed the upward price spiral, one cause of the rise of multifamily housing today.

Designs for many of these early speculative houses and their neighborhoods were not impressive and often bordered on monotony. Yet over the years their understated forms and consistent use of materials have served as a marvelous backdrop for Texas pecans and wisteria and azaleas. Smooth lawns of Bermuda grass and St. Augustine, walls of pyracantha, beds of day lilies, zinnias, dogwood, and jessamine are now characteristic of Dallas' postwar developments.

Building materials used in this speculative housing were generally local products, especially pine framing from East Texas timber and bricks manufactured in Denton and Mineral Wells. Designs originated more from East Coast styles and European architecture than from Spanish influences within the Southwest. Dallas has always been the one Texas city with a closer affinity in style to the East and Europe than to the West. (As an aside, the stone and timber houses usually found farther south in Texas also are not of Spanish origin. These were the work of early skilled German or French stone masons who settled throughout the Hill Country.) Exterior Spanish stucco finishes were not widely used in Dallas until the end of the 1960s when bricks became too costly for some developers' budgets. Another unique quirk of the Dallas housing market of the 1960s was the continual construction of speculative houses costing well over $100,000 (and sometimes $200,000). In Dallas these houses gener-

OPPOSITE, ABOVE: Highland Park Village. BELOW: Red Bird Mall. The oldest and newest of Dallas' shopping centers.

ally have the same materials and forms as other less expensive housing, only they are bigger and have larger lots. They are usually priced solely by size, not on a basis of design quality or unique workmanship—controversial designs might be hard to resell.

Almost as dramatic as the boom in single-family housing in the 1945–60 era was the beginning in the middle 1960s of another social phenomenon: the desire of young single people to get together and to live a changing life-style. The elderly found home ownership and maintenance too troublesome and too expensive; many opted for apartments. And a demographic change in the make-up of Dallas population was brought about, in part, by the seemingly endless influx of young people to take jobs in banks, insurance companies, and the burgeoning Collins and Texas Instruments electronic industries that had suddenly grown into giant companies with a type of employment that suited young people.

All these things set off a wave of apartment building, first in the fashionable older areas along Gaston Avenue in East Dallas, then in Oak Lawn and along Zang Boulevard in Oak Cliff. The appetite for apartments appeared insatiable.

Early speculative apartments were often two-story units with central corridors, building types common in the northern portions of the United States. Soon developers switched to garden apartments with central courtyards, extensive landscaping, and private pools. The race for amenities began. The garden idea, indigenous to the Southwest, was a powerful sales tool in Dallas, the "utilitarian city."

Older buildings soon became obsolete in design and in the services offered long before they were fully depreciated or their mortgages expired. There simply was no end to extra amenities that could be found as apartments became competitive— private club memberships, tennis, golf, buses to the football games, and some apartments even offered private limousine service as a special appeal to the "airline stewardess" set.

Apartment living may have peaked with the Village (1970–77), a fully self-contained project with 3,300 apartments located near the heart of North Dallas. In addition to its nineteen swimming pools and extensive landscaping, it has its own golf course, tennis center, recreational club and restaurant, playing fields, and a wide range of personal services. Complete with a small adjacent specialty shopping center, it is essentially a total village housing eight thousand people. But sidewalks lead to parking lots, and everyone drives to the central club.

High-rise housing and town-house developments have been slow to fire the imagination of Southwesterners. Although several high-rise experiments such as the prominent 3525 Turtle Creek Tower (1957) were planned as apartments, most have successfully converted to condominiums in recent years. Similarly, new town-house developments in Oak Lawn and North Dallas are beginning to sell more quickly. Perhaps these trends indicate today's new families fresh from apartment living are opting for housing more akin to their former life-styles rather than those of their parents.

TODAY AND TOMORROW

Dallas' real estate market today is characterized by many disturbing and difficult conditions. In the late 1960s a plentiful supply of low-interest rate funds (cheap money) fanned speculative flames and encouraged many new people to build housing estates, apartments, warehouses, and industrial buildings. Following them were traffickers in land syndication. Each transfer of property saw land prices climb—in all too many cases until it was too expensive to be used by developers. Today development problems are compounded by overpriced capital. Available capital for real estate development is at such a high interest rate that many projects cannot get started. Apartments are showing vacancies far above the level of profitable operations. Single-family housing is suffering as contractors and buyers are unable to qualify for loans or mortgages.

Dallas, in 1976, is oversupplied with office space, and vast amounts, particularly downtown, stand vacant. The downtown area as a retailing center has lost some of its appeal with the arrival of the mall shopping centers. Parking is difficult and expensive, and in contrast with the suburban centers there is no order or unity of retail purpose. New regional centers have provided a veritable necklace of "nodes" around the Central Business District. Each offers its own unique pattern of retail and sometimes office uses. If these outlying areas continue to grow, further changes in the use of nearby residential and commercial real estate will surely be seen. The Central Business District may well become what Wall Street is to New York or "the City" is to London, a specialized financial district in use only six to eight hours each day.

Yet Dallas has apparently reached a finite size. It has grown in almost all directions, to the borders of strong new towns with their own identity and goals. This regional separateness has sometimes brought about conflict, duplication, higher public costs, poorer building quality, and lost opportunities for an urban framework designed for the common good. Consequently, the city's attentions today are primarily focused on maintaining and improving Dallas services—utilities, roads, education and parks—to nearly one million residents over its three-hundred square miles. The task of continuing the development of Dallas as a world capital will be a qualitative one in the future, not one of quantity.

Certain projects offer a glimpse of Dallas' urban future and its chances of becoming such a world city. One of these, residential in character, is Temple Emanu-El on the city's early outer loop, Northwest Highway. Completed in 1957 by local architects Max Sandfield and Howard Meyer, the project's use of local materials and an open flowing site plan is very representative of the Southwest. Their handsome design was further reinforced by the skillful work of local landscape designers and nationally known artists so that today it has become a classic architectural statement. A second notable project is the newer Park Central Development, a three-hundred-acre development fifteen miles from the Central Business District. Its setting is parklike, and it includes medical, entertainment, and sports facilities, offices, retail businesses, and hotels. With such a scope it could become far more than an alternate to the Central Business District. Similar to Crown Center in Kansas City, it is big enough to develop its own internal environment. And it may one day suggest a new direction in combinations of land uses.

On a larger scale, Park Central combined with nearby Texas Instruments (1958) will create another major business and employment center. With the city's major retail center, NorthPark, midway between it and the original Central Business District, North Central Expressway may now become the "central spine" of a New Dallas, a linear center extending ten to twelve miles. Reinforcing this pattern are the glass-walled office developments of NorthPark and Campbell Center at the mid-point and numerous other office towers and hotels located at each crossroad throughout its length. Also, the expressway's parallel improved roadway, Greenville Avenue, in one instance one block away, is fast becoming the city's restaurant and entertainment center. The notorious bars, saloons, and gambling halls on downtown Main Street in the late 1800s originally gave Dallas its reputation as a significant place among many struggling settlements. Although not as wild or open as those earlier examples, Greenville Avenue's residents now contribute that richness and humanity necessary in a "downtown" today, despite their lack of centrality. This evolving "urban spine" form of growth in Dallas may have analogies in other cities such as Wilshire Boulevard's growth in Los Angeles; and mass transit lines are now being planned in both cities.

Two significant developments have recently occurred outside the city, and these have yet to be fully appreciated. The first, the Dallas–Fort Worth Regional Airport

(1975), is a good example of both system building and a powerful design in which careful attention was paid to every detail within the viewer's eye. Covering 17,500 acres, the new regional airport should not only improve air travel within the region but also unite the political interests of all participating municipalities. The airport's role as a forum and that of the young North Texas Council of Governments are essential if we are to create an effective and productive regional approach to government.

The second, the Dallas County Community College System, is discussed elsewhere in more detail by its administrator. Briefly, the system's completion of its first four campuses in 1972 is of equal architectural and political significance to the airport. The system's use of bold design, creative local educational opportunities, and cohesive political exercises required to create the county-wide campuses will continue to have a profound effect on the county and city's future.

Dallas' real estate future will be one of refining and emphasizing its existing neighborhoods and centers, either central or suburban. Forces of expansion will be rechanneled into forces of redevelopment. As in 1910, the technologies are in place, the roads are known, and only the quality of urban life we are seeking needs to be decided. The strictly utilitarian approach to the city's growth has ended—maybe.

Perhaps a strong design idea such as Town Lake, repeatedly proposed throughout the city's history, will be necessary to stimulate the downtown's resurgence. Such a scheme would simultaneously provide vistas, water, and shore-front parks—all dynamic and invaluable ingredients to a city center now void of almost all such amenities. Historically, in this landscape, access to water has always had an almost sacred appeal.

Preservation of the physical character of Dallas should be well thought out. In many ways, the remodeling of the downtown Sanger Building for El Centro College's use is an excellent example of historical preservation—retaining the character of the past, while benefiting the future of the city.

The city's present Land Use Plan is a thoughtful program for remaining land both in the inner city and in areas close to the center. On the assumption the future may hold a different character from what we have seen in the past, we can expect to see good public schools coming back into the inner city area. This action will be extremely significant to housing patterns. One may also expect to see cluster homes, patio homes, and apartments following the schools into the inner city. Public and private sectors must co-operate in the use of increasingly precious space to foster a spirit of urbanization that will be humanistically oriented. The end results sought by such developments will be places found in some European cities, where living, working, and playing conditions occur within a useful limited area. Fortunately, in 1970 the city's census did indicate that its density, a historic measure of the human interaction afforded by urban environments, is on the rise after declining for the past thirty years. It is now at 4.5 people per acre, equivalent to when electric streetcars were first put into use in 1890.

Economic vitality, reflected by the real estate industry, will be dependent upon the city's response to the development of mass transportation, cultural and educational facilities, the arts, housing, and other major social issues. Real estate development may never be as profitable as it was in the fifties and sixties. High interest rates, availability of land, national inflation, cost of labor and materials, and energy shortages are all components of the future equation that did not exist at that time. Yet momentary conditions must not be viewed as road blocks to future real estate development. If envisioned real estate ventures truly offer solutions to real and lasting human needs, a time will come when they are affordable. Yet only those entrepreneurs with great clarity of foresight, flexibility, patience, and commitment will weather extensive delays. This sorting factor is often necessary in any evolutionary process to create the best. It is often said that "the visionary dreams of one generation can become the routine accomplishments of another." Many of the visions of the leaders of the fifties and sixties have now been accomplished.

Today's men and women of leadership, serving the citizens of Dallas, have a new challenge determined by a very different set of parameters. How we respond is the question that will determine the form of Dallas tomorrow, and its place in the nation's future urban growth.

The first member of the Overton family arrived in Dallas in 1844; he was W. P. Overton, who became a landowner and operated the first gristmill in Dallas County. Although W. W. Overton, Jr., was born in Kansas City, Kansas, in 1897, he grew up in Dallas and attended Metropolitan Business College and later the University of Texas in Austin. During his early years most of his time was spent working for his father in the sugar business in Dallas.

After business ventures in San Antonio and El Paso, Mr. Overton settled permanently in Dallas with his interest concentrated in the Texas Bank and Trust Company since 1942. He was chairman of the board from 1943 to 1971, chairman of the executive committee from 1971 to 1974, and remains a director.

His work as trustee, chairman, and now life councilor of the Conference Board, an organization of four thousand chief executive officers of major national and international business, has been an important part of his business activites for over a quarter of a century.

In 1960 Mr. Overton provided Columbia University with a research grant to study the city's central area problem of blight. The "Columbia Plan" for Dallas was the result, and many of its recommendations were incorporated into the exemplary Main Place development and were later adopted by the city of Dallas as its planning precepts for the downtown district.

Mr. Overton has served as national fund chairman of the American Red Cross and chairman of the International Red Cross Committee. He was a founder of the Central Business District Association of Dallas and the Caruth Memorial Rehabilitation Institute and has been a trustee and/or director of the Trinity Improvement Association, Greater Dallas Planning Council, Southwestern Medical Foundation, Texas Research Foundation, State Fair of Texas, Dallas Theater Center, and Dallas Citizens Council. He was president of the Chamber of Commerce, and his many other interests include the United Fund, YMCA, Dallas Historical Society, Dallas Heritage Society, and Boys Club of Dallas.

He was married to the former Evelyn Lucas, of Dallas. The late Mrs. Overton was chairman of the Southwest Hospitality Board of the Metropolitan Grand Opera Association.

Finance

by W. W. OVERTON, JR.

Sometime in the 1880s, Jay Gould, the railroad magnate, remarked on the future of Dallas, "I expect to see Dallas a city of 250,000 people." I applaud his prophecy, inasmuch as the current population is over a million. During the 133 years since its first settlement, Dallas has developed from a cluster of log cabins on the frontier of Texas to the eighth largest city in the nation. It is the financial center of the Southwest, and for better or worse, Dallas is the image of the people who made it. It is a forward, energetic city whose growth is due to the character of its people, and not to chance or location. Dallas is what it is because the leaders of Dallas planned it that way!

During the first decade of Dallas, money in the form of hard cash did not often change hands. Spanish silver or gold was probably the medium of exchange when purchases were made in other cities, but for ordinary transactions among the settlers, goods were usually bartered. Buffalo hides were traded for manufactured goods, and wheat and corn for flour and meal.

At the outbreak of the Civil War, Dallas was achieving recognition as a growing trade center and each week brought new pioneers from Kentucky, Missouri, Ohio, Georgia, Mississippi, Alabama, and especially Tennessee. Dallas was the center of a fertile farming area with wheat the first source of wealth, to be followed later by cattle, cotton, and oil. During the Civil War it was selected as one of the important foodstuff bases of the Confederate Army.

There were no banks in Dallas until after the Civil War, and the people of Texas were generally opposed to the chartering of banks. During this time, the merchants often acted as bankers, with the larger transactions handled directly by individuals. As more money flowed into Dallas, the early pioneers left their money with merchants they trusted, and the merchants often used discarded lard cans hanging from the ceiling to hold the money left with them. In those days each man had faith in each other, and no receipts were given and no records kept! However, the financial needs of the people gradually created a demand for a more convenient and stable form of exchange, and the private individuals and merchants supplying these needs were commonly known as moneylenders.

BANKING

The real history of banking in Dallas begins in the late 1860s with the establishment of private banks. It is believed that the first banking house in the city was the private firm of Gaston and Camp, located on the southeast corner of Main and Jefferson on the courthouse square. It was organized in 1868 by Captain William H. Gaston and Aaron C. Camp, with Captain Gaston putting a capital of twenty thousand gold dollars into the business. Private banking was apparently very casual during this period, and the money left by the depositors was simply marked with their name and put in an iron safe. On demand, the same money was returned to the depositor with no charge for the service! Loans were made from the partners' capital.

In the same year another private banking firm was formed by T. C. Jordan and A. G. Mays under the name of T. C. Jordan and Company. A few years later, Colonel W. E. Hughes, J. R. Couts, and Colonel C. C. Slaughter, a wealthy West Texas cattleman, purchased the bank, and it opened for business in 1873 as the City Bank of Dallas. (The First National Bank in Dallas, at the present time one of the largest banks in the Southwest, traces its lineage back to these first two private banks established in Dallas.) The casual nature of banking in those early days reminds me of an elderly West Texas cattleman who moved to Dallas for his retirement many years ago. Needing a safe place to deposit all his money, he opened a small private bank in a hole in the wall in the lower downtown section of Dallas. He had one girl to take care of the books and the letter writing, and a big desk by the front window where he could watch the people pass on their way to town. One day one of his West Texas cronies was in Dallas on business. He was walking down Main Street when he happened to pass the bank and, to his surprise, saw the old cattleman sitting at the desk. He went in.

OPPOSITE: Banks reflecting banks. In the mirrorlike façade of the First International Building can be seen the Mercantile National Bank with its clock tower, on the left; the First National Bank, in the center foreground; and on the right, with a modernistic spire, the Republic National Bank.

"What're you doing here, Jim?" he said in greeting.

"I'm doing business," said the old cattleman with the measured caution that the occasion demanded. "I'm in the banking business. This here is a bank."

"Oh, come on, Jim," joshed the friend, "you don't know anything about banking."

The old-timer looked at him through narrowed eyelids. "Oh no?" he replied. "Well, you just try to borrow some money, and see!"

Dallas was now a full-fledged outpost town at the three forks of the Trinity River with its streets swarming with cowboys and pioneers headed westward. Herds of cattle bound northward over the Chisholm Trail bawled lustily as their hoofs raised great clouds of dust in the streets. Sweating ox teams hauled heavy wagons loaded with buffalo hides into town, and hauled out equally heavy loads of provisions and supplies. Husky teamsters and swaggering cowboys surged up and down the streets, spending their money with easy freedom on food and entertainment.

With the coming of the railroads in 1872, this hustling and bustling frontier town entered into a new period of rapid growth and economic expansion. The newly constructed railroads brought thousands of immigrants into Texas, and the rapid expansion of trade encouraged the organization of many banks, both private and national.

By 1891 the National Bank of Commerce, which was organized in 1889, consolidated with the private bank of Flippen, Adoue and Lobit (founded in 1878) and has the distinction of being the only bank established in Dallas in the nineteenth century that has retained the same name from that time to the present. During the panic of 1893, J. B. Adoue, president of the bank, had not only indomitable courage but a keen sense of humor. The story is recounted that when a depositor from another bank approached Mr. Adoue in the lobby of the National Bank of Commerce with the money he had withdrawn from this other bank, stating that he wanted to open an account, Mr. Adoue shook his finger in the man's face and speaking in a loud tone of voice so that everyone in the bank would hear him, said, "Take your account back to your own bank. That bank is as strong as wheat and the Rock of Gibraltar, but this bank is busted!" A hush fell over the lobby for a moment, followed by a ripple of laughter. This calm, clear-eyed banker knew that nothing destroys fear so quickly as laughter.

International banking in Dallas must have begun in July 1893 when Mr. B. Adoue, brother of J. B. Adoue, inserted an advertisement in the *News* announcing the firm of "Adoue & Lobit, Bankers and Commission Merchants. Sight drafts on London, Berlin, Paris, Stockholm, Bremen, Hamburg, and Frankfort."

In spite of periods of depression, the last few years of the century were fairly uneventful for Dallas business. Dallas continued to show the rapid growth characteristic of cities in the newer sections of the country. At the turn of the century, Dallas had only six banks: the National Bank of Dallas, City National Bank,

American National Bank, National Exchange Bank, National Bank of Commerce, and the private firm of Gaston and Gaston (which was later to become part of Republic National Bank of Dallas).

In the year 1900, significant changes were made in the financial structure within the nation. In March an act was finally passed and signed that insured the gold standard by providing that all forms of money must be redeemable in gold. In 1900 Dallas had a population of 42,000 and was upon the threshold of an era of unprecedented expansion. A new bill became law in 1905 permitting the organization of state banks, and on August 15, 1905, the First State Bank made its appearance in Dallas (absorbed by Security National Bank in 1919).

The businessmen of Dallas found that by working together they could get things done, and they began a pattern of aggressive, cohesive business leadership that guided Dallas from a frontier town to a modern, sophisticated city. With only dirt roads leading to the nearby towns, a hundred-mile interurban system was inaugurated leading north to Denison and Sherman, and south through the various towns to Waco. The interurban would stop in the center of each town, and to promote business in downtown Dallas, the Chamber of Commerce organized weekly trade trips to these towns by Dallas businessmen. Carrying walking canes and wearing straw hats with "Welcome to Dallas" on the headbands, they would parade up and down the central section of each town. By the close of 1906, Dallas was the banking center of the state. Dallas banks furnished a major portion of the funds necessary to move the Texas cotton crop, and Dallas exchange was accepted at par in all cities of the Southwest. To the cotton and wheat farmers, the cattlemen and the oilmen, Dallas had bankers willing to stake a man, and firms eager to insure him. The pattern was set—Dallas was looking to the future, and its businessmen went on to tap the wealth of the state by servicing it.

The year 1914 represents an important date in the history of banking in Dallas. Many business and financial leaders undertook a strenuous campaign to have Dallas designated as the regional bank representing the Federal Reserve System. At a general mass meeting held in Dallas on January 18, an executive committee was formed to direct the campaign. At the beginning of the Dallas committee's activities, it was decided that the first and most important step was the consummation of an agreement with representatives of other Texas cities seeking the regional bank in order to present a solid front for a reserve bank in Texas first—and work for the location of the bank in their own respective cities next.

The next move on the part of the Dallas leaders was to ascertain the strongest point in favor of Dallas as the location for the bank. At a special hearing held in Austin by Secretary of the Treasury William G. McAdoo and Secretary of Agriculture David F. Houston, it was found that committees from other cities were there also, including Fort Worth, Houston, San Antonio, Oklahoma City, El Paso, and New Orleans. As no decision was made at the close of this hearing, arrangements

Some fifty years ago these men attended a luncheon at the Baker Hotel hosted by the Dallas Clearing House Association and Dallas Rotary Club to honor J. F. T. O'Connor, Comptroller of the Currency, and Jesse H. Jones, Chairman of the Reconstruction Finance Corporation.

SEATED LEFT TO RIGHT: Jesse H. Jones, R. L. Thornton, Sr., Nathan Adams, J. F. T. O'Connor, Fred Florence.

STANDING FIRST ROW: B. A. McKinney, C. C. Walsh, Warren Andrews, R. F. Siddons, R. R. Gilbert, J. D. Gillespie, Marshall R. Diggs, Lang Wharton, George B. Dealey.

BACK ROW: Harry A. Olmstead, J. B. Adoue, George Matthews, R. D. Suddarth, Joe E. Lawther, Mayor Charles E. Turner, Leslie Waggener, W. M. Williams, R. H. Collier, George Fix, W. A. Philpott, Jr. COURTESY OF R. L. THORNTON, JR.

Colonel W. E. Hughes

Captain W. H. Thomas
FRANK ROGERS

Captain William H. Gaston
FRANK ROGERS

W. O. Connor

John the Baptist Adoue, Jr.
FRANK ROGERS

Fred Florence
BLANK-STOLLER

R. H. Stewart
BLANK-STOLLER

Nathan Adams
G. ALLEN LAINSON STUDIOS

Karl Hoblitzelle was born in St. Louis in 1879, one of thirteen children. He rose from office boy to Director of Works at the St. Louis World's Fair and then was appointed to direct its demolition. In 1905 he brought his savings of $2,500 to Dallas to open the Interstate Amusement Company with theaters in Dallas, Fort Worth, Waco, and San Antonio, presenting vaudeville and then motion pictures as the company evolved into one of the nation's major distribution circuits. Mr. Hoblitzelle's interests and philanthropies were multiple, centering mainly on the Texas Research Foundation, the Dallas Museum of Fine Arts, the University of Texas Southwestern Medical School, Hoblitzelle Foundation, Southern Methodist University, and Baylor Hospital. He was married to Esther Thomas, of Louisville, Kentucky, actress and recording artist known professionally as Esther Walker. Mr. Hoblitzelle died in 1967. LEE LANGUM.

A cowboy on his father's ranch in Sabine County, Texas, and a Confederate Army officer, Colonel C. C. Slaughter came to Dallas in 1873. Here he established his own cattle company, invested in real estate, and became involved in the organization of local banking. His financial support of Baylor University and Baylor Hospital met many early needs in education and hospital care development and set an example for his peers in the rapidly growing city. He was married to Sarah Anne Jowell, also of Sabine County. Colonel Slaughter died in 1919.

Karl Hoblitzelle, Amon Carter, of Fort Worth, and R. L. Thornton, Sr., at a Texas Research Foundation banquet in May 1952. COURTESY OF R. L. THORNTON, JR.

1916 bank at 704 Main Street converted by its officers from what had been the Blue Goose Restaurant next to Blue Goose Saloon. This bank was a forerunner of the Mercantile National. COURTESY OF R. L. THORTON, JR.

were made for delegations of Dallas men to visit Secretary McAdoo, Controller John S. Williams, Secretary Houston, Postmaster General Albert S. Burleson, and President Woodrow Wilson to continue their efforts. Because of the rivalry between the various cities, a code was worked out whereby confidential information from Washington could be relayed to Dallas businessmen through George B. Dealey, publisher of the Dallas *Morning News*. One such telegram sent to Mr. Dealey was as follows:

DELIGHTFUL[1] IN NO DANGER OF FLORAL[2] BUT HANDICAP[3] THREATENING. WIRE MERCURY[4] DATA SHOWING DELIGHTFUL[1] MORE DESIRABLE THAN HANDICAP[3]. THINK TACITUS[5] MAKING TROUBLE BUT MERCURY[4] DEPENDING ON ALLAH[6]. ALL STRICT-EST CONFIDENCE.

1. Dallas	4. Albert Burleson
2. Fort Worth	5. Col. E. M. House*
3. Houston	6. Woodrow Wilson

Decoded message:

DALLAS IN NO DANGER OF FORT WORTH BUT HOUSTON THREATENING. WIRE ALBERT BURLESON DATA SHOWING DAL-LAS MORE DESIRABLE THAN HOUSTON. THINK COL. E. M. HOUSE MAKING TROUBLE BUT ALBERT BURLESON DEPENDING ON WOODROW WILSON. ALL STRICTEST CONFIDENCE.

Finally, on April 2, 1914, Dallas was chosen over other cities because it had shown the greatest economic growth in the preceding decade and so was awarded the Federal Reserve Bank for the Eleventh District. The bank opened on November 16 of the same year and named E. O. Tenison, president of the City National Bank, as its first chairman. The Eleventh District includes all of Texas and parts of New Mexico, Louisiana, Oklahoma, and Arizona. Branches were later established in Houston, El Paso, and San Antonio. Among the financial men who deserved much of the credit for securing the bank for Dallas were J. Howard Ardrey, cashier of City National Bank and president of the Dallas Clearing House; Royal Ferris, president of the American Exchange Bank; Nathan Adams, vice-president of the American Exchange Bank and president of the Texas Bankers Association; and Rhodes S. Baker, an attorney who was later to help organize the Dallas Federal Savings and Loan Association.

In 1917 the Dallas County State Bank was organized. That organization, which had begun a year previously as the private banking firm of Stiles, Thornton, and Lund, is an important event in Dallas banking. It centers around R. L. Thornton, a successful candy salesman from Hillsboro, who became not only a great banker but also a great civic leader. When the private bank was founded, Bob Thornton and

*Confidential adviser to President Woodrow Wilson living in Austin.

his friends managed to get together $20,000 capital and find a set of old fixtures which they bought for $350. Next, they rented a room at 704 Main Street which was formerly occupied by Nathan Kaufman's Blue Goose Saloon and Restaurant, revarnished the fixtures themselves, whitewashed the walls, and opened their doors to the public. The Dallas County Bank later became the Mercantile National Bank at Dallas, which ranks among the largest banks in the nation.

The Guaranty Bank and Trust Company received its charter in 1920 and was known as the "Day and Night Bank" because its doors were open daily from 9 A.M. until 8 P.M. and on Saturdays from 9 A.M. until 10 P.M. This new bank with its unusual hours attracted many customers and within a month announced it had twelve hundred new customers with a total of $900,000 in deposits. Its first president was Tom M. Dees, who soon became chairman of the board. He was followed by W. O. Connor, formerly credit manager of Sanger Brothers.

By 1928 the financial leaders in Dallas, aware that Dallas was becoming an industrial and financial center, formed an organization to put on an intensive drive to secure for Dallas new industries, branch sales offices of national concerns, branch factories, and branch distribution offices. This organization was called Industrial Dallas, Inc., and R. L. Thornton, president of the Mercantile National Bank, was the president. A fund of $500,000 was raised by subscription among the banks and business houses in Dallas to finance a four-year campaign, and during these four years more than a thousand new businesses were established in Dallas. To the work of this organization can be attributed much of the current growth of Dallas.

There were many consolidations and name changes in early Dallas banking, but two of the most important took place in 1929. The City National Bank and the American Exchange National Bank consolidated to form the First National Bank in Dallas, thus making it the largest bank in the Eleventh Federal Reserve District at that time. Some of the officers of the two combined banks were Henry C. Coke, chairman of the board, R. H. Stewart, vice-chairman of the board, and Nathan Adams, president. The other merger of great importance was the Republic National Bank and the North Texas National Bank. This merger made the Republic National Bank the second largest in Dallas. The combined officers of this merger were W. O. Connor, chairman of the board, Wirt Davis, vice-chairman of the board, and Fred F. Florence, president.

During the twenties, Dallas inevitably felt the current national and international economic events. Dallas bankers and businessmen experienced the boom years in the early twenties and the stock market crash in 1929. The full effect of the stock market crash was not realized at first in Dallas, but by 1930 it was revealed that bank deposits had declined nearly $9.5 million and that unemployment had become such a problem that an Emergency Unemployment Relief Committee was set up under the chairmanship of R. L. Thornton and other top business leaders.

Although these were unpredictable times, the Texas Bank and Trust Company opened its doors for business as a subsidiary of Mercantile Bank and Trust (now the

Mercantile National Bank at Dallas) on January 3, 1930, at the corner of Main and Lamar streets. R. L. Thornton, one of the organizers of the bank, was chairman of the board. The new bank occupied the old quarters of the Mercantile, and the Mercantile moved to the new quarters it had leased in the Magnolia Building. The Texas Bank was organized because it was felt that an institution in the west portion of the metropolitan district would be needed after the removal of the Mercantile National Bank from this section of town, which was in the midst of the wholesale and retail districts. In the early 1940s the area served by the Texas Bank did not appear to have a very promising future, and the Mercantile National decided it would be wiser to concentrate on their more profitable business activities elsewhere. To this end they offered the management and majority stockholders of the Texas Bank the opportunity to buy the controlling interest of the bank. I had bought twenty-five shares of stock in 1930 and was elected to the board of directors in 1936. Although my father and I were sugar brokers in Texas, it seemed to me that there was a tremendous future for the Texas Bank if it could be operated with aggressiveness and enthusiasm, and I decided to negotiate with the Mercantile Bank. In 1943 the control of the bank passed to me and my associates. We felt that a policy of aggressive selling, seeking new markets, expanding services, and providing convenience for the customer would be the key to success, and to implement this market-oriented strategy we began searching for a new president. Randall Gilbert, president of Federal Reserve Bank at that time, recommended to me that a top bond man be considered and suggested P. B. (Jack) Garrett.

One afternoon in 1944, I went out to Brookhollow Golf Club to meet Jack for a game of golf. During the game, however, I kept remembering that I was looking for a president for Texas Bank and realized that Jack was the right man for the job. So I began, "Jack, you knew we purchased the Texas Bank earlier this year. It's been doing very well and we believe it has a great future, but we are still looking for the right man to take over its presidency. I think you would be great for the position. Will you come with us, Jack?" Jack was stunned, and neither of us said anything for a few minutes. Jack finally replied, "Bill, thanks for your confidence in me, but I am not a banker, as you well know. I'm a bond man, and the banking business is quite different from the bond business."

"Jack, I'm a sugar man. I'm not a banker either. Think it over." And by the end of 1944, both of us nonbankers—one a sugar man and one a bond man—were deeply immersed in the banking business, and we then established a bond department and a correspondent bank department.

While Dallas was experiencing a growth rate far greater than the nation as a whole, Texas Bank and Trust Company was growing at a faster rate than any other bank in the five-state Southwest area, and is presently the fourth largest bank in Dallas.

Tracing the history of the First National Bank in Dallas involves approximately eighteen name changes and consolidations. Nathan Adams served as the first president from 1929 to 1944, and later as board chairman. Arriving in Dallas from

Original board of directors, 1914, Federal Reserve Bank of Dallas. On first step right to left: Marion Sansom, Fort Worth; Frank Kell, Wichita Falls.
MIDDLE ROW RIGHT TO LEFT: E. O. Tenison, Dallas; Felix Martinez, El Paso; Oscar Well, Houston.
BACK ROW RIGHT TO LEFT: J. J. Culbertson, Paris; E. K. Smith, Shreveport; B. A. McKinney, Durant. Absent was W. F. McCaleb, San Antonio. COURTESY OF THE FEDERAL RESERVE BANK OF DALLAS.

Tennessee in 1889, he became president of American Exchange National Bank. Nate Adams stayed on to develop the First National into a leading bank in the Southwest and, in addition to his banking responsibilities, was an important civic leader. Following Nathan Adams as president was Edgar L. Flippen, who held that office until 1950, when Ben Wooten succeeded him. In 1972 the First International Bancshares was organized with Robert H. Stewart III as chairman of the board and W. Dewey Presley as president, the positions they had previously held with First National before the holding company was formed. Harry A. Shuford is now chairman of the board of First National Bank and Elvis L. Mason is president.

Mr. Stewart, by the way, is a third-generation banker in Dallas. His father was a director of the First National Bank and his grandfather had been vice-chairman of the board.

The Republic National Bank in Dallas also has a long history of mergers and name changes. W. O. Connor was chairman of the board from 1929 until his death in 1934, and Fred F. Florence was president during this time. Mr. Connor had become associated with Fred years before when he was president of the Guaranty Bank and Trust Company and trying to increase the capital of the bank by $1 million. At that time Fred Florence was president of the Alto State Bank in East

Texas. He called Mr. Connor and told him that he had a customer at his bank in East Texas who wanted to buy $25,000 worth of stock in Connor's bank. Connor, of course, was delighted. Fred next advised Connor that he had received the $25,000 and had opened an account in his own bank for that amount in the name of the Guaranty Bank and Trust Company. Right then, Connor sensed in Fred Florence a quick mind, useful in banking and serving customers, and offered him a job in his own bank as first vice-president and director. Fred, of course, accepted and later was active at Republic Bank as president and chairman of the executive committee from 1929 until his death in 1960. He was president of the American Bankers Association in 1955–56 and was active in many civic endeavors.

Another important man in the history of Republic Bank and Dallas was Karl Hoblitzelle. Karl became a director of the bank in 1929 and was chairman of the board from 1945 to 1965. Originally from St. Louis, he was a theater magnate, a financier, and a philanthropist. Because of his deep concern for humanity, his words are set in bronze at the Ervay Street entrance to the Republic National Bank Building:

THIS BUILDING IS DEDICATED TO THE PRINCIPLE

THAT NO INSTITUTION CAN LONG ENDURE

UNLESS IT SERVES FAITHFULLY AND UNSELFISHLY

ITS COUNTRY, ITS STATE AND ITS COMMUNITY

In 1974 the Republic National Bank formed a holding company called the Republic of Texas Corporation. James W. Aston, who had been president and chairman of the board of Republic National Bank before the holding company was formed, is now chairman of the board of the holding company and James D. Berry is president. James W. Keay is chairman of the board at Republic Bank and Charles H. Pistor, Jr., is president.

The Mercantile National Bank at Dallas is the third largest bank in Dallas today and formed the Mercantile Texas Corporation, a holding company, with R. L. Thornton, Jr., as chairman and Gene H. Bishop as president and chief executive officer. Bob Thornton followed in his father's footsteps as a banker until his recent retirement as chairman of the board. Chief among his civic interests has been the Dallas County Community College District. He has served as chairman of the board of trustees since its inception ten years ago. Bob Thornton's leadership provided funds for the construction of three colleges and a substantial part of a fourth through the execution of a bond issue of $15 million at $3\frac{3}{8}$ per cent and another bond issue of $26.5 million at 4.30 per cent. There remains a continuing project with two more colleges under construction and one still in the planning stage.

Since the early days of banking in Dallas, the banks have grown in size from the small private banks in 1868 to among the top twenty-five in the nation today. Our banks have remained strong throughout their history, and although there have been national crises during these years, such as world wars and depressions, Dallas banks have always retained the confidence of their customers. As they have grown in size, they have increased their services and have given Dallas a solid financial base. The number of banks has increased considerably also. In 1894—more than eighty years ago—Dallas had five banks, with total deposits of about $3 million. As of December 31, 1975, Dallas had fifty-three banks and total deposits of more than $10 billion.

The research department of the Federal Reserve Bank in Dallas reported that earnings of the Dallas banks nearly doubled from 1969 to 1974. The dynamic growth the Southwest has enjoyed during this period is also reflected in the figures released by the Federal Deposit Insurance Corporation for 1974 which ranks the Dallas-Fort Worth area eighth in commercial bank deposits (and the Houston area ninth) among the nation's twenty most populous Standard Metropolitan Statistical Areas.

SAVINGS AND LOAN ASSOCIATIONS

The forerunners of our present savings and loan associations were known as building societies and were first established in England around 1780. These were established primarily for the accumulation of savings and the issuance of home loans. In the United States the first savings and loan association was in Frankfurt, Pennsylvania, in 1831. The first loan was made to a village lamplighter whose home still stands in Philadelphia. These were voluntary associations which usually consisted of one hundred men who agreed to pay ten dollars per month for one hundred months. At that time a single-family home cost about one thousand dollars, and at each meeting of the association a drawing would be held to see which member would be the lucky winner to get the thousand dollars to build his home. After each member had built his home, the association would be dissolved. Later these associations were incorporated and followed the corporation laws of each state.

There were mutual savings and loan associations established in Dallas as early as 1880 and among these were Dallas Homestead and Loan Association, Sanger Brothers Employee's Association, and Dallas Gas and Fuel Company's Employee's Loan Association.

Interestingly, savings and loan associations in Dallas were often started by real estate and insurance agencies. A desk in the back room of the agency would be the beginning of the savings and loan, with the real estate or the insurance business the main income, and the savings and loan only a side line.

One evening after a prayer meeting at the First Presbyterian Church in Dallas, E. E. Shelton and some of his friends stood on the steps of the church and began making plans to organize a new savings and loan. This was the beginning of the Dallas Building and Loan Association, which was founded in 1919 by Ed Shelton. He joined forces with Rhodes S. Baker, who became the first president, and J. G. Loving, who became secretary and treasurer. Their first office space was on Commerce Street where the Century Room of the Adolphus Hotel is now located. Some years later, while Ed Shelton was president, they were granted a federal charter and changed their name to the present one, which is the Dallas Federal Savings and Loan Association. They are the oldest savings and loan in Dallas and also the largest in Texas, with fourteen branch offices and new corporate headquarters in Preston Center. In 1958 Lloyd S. Bowles, Sr., was made president, with Ed Shelton remaining as chairman of the board until his death in 1964. At that time, Ben H. Wooten, who had retired as chairman of the board at First National Bank in Dallas, was named chairman of the board.

Upon his graduation from North Texas State University, Ben had entered the banking field for a short time, but later became chief examiner for the Federal Home Loan Banking System. From 1932 until 1953 he served as chairman of the board and president of the Federal Home Loan Bank at Little Rock, Arkansas. While still holding this position, he became president of First National Bank from 1950 to 1960 and was elevated to chairman of the board until his retirement in 1963. A modest man, he was often quoted as saying he was born on a farm near Timpson in East Texas "on RFD #4, Box 22 to be exact." Upon Ben's death in 1971, Lloyd Bowles assumed the offices of both board chairman and president of Dallas Federal Savings and Loan and in 1975 was national president of the U. S. League of Savings Associations. According to Thomas S. Walker, a long-time director, the assets of Dallas Federal increased from $202,000 in 1920 to $818,680,000 at the close of 1975.

By 1925 other building and loan associations had been established, including the present First Federal Savings and Loan Association and the Guardian Savings and Loan Association. Later, in 1932 the Metropolitan Savings and Loan was formed with J. B. Adoue, Jr., president.

The nationwide depression of 1929 brought about many changes, and from this period the present system of supervision of savings and loans developed. Specific and definite efforts were made to improve the corporate image of savings and loans. The Federal Home Loan Bank System was established in July 1932, and the first board met with Nathan Adams (president of First National Bank) as a member from Dallas. The Federal Savings and Loan Insurance Corporation was also established at this time.

In 1946 the Oak Cliff Savings and Loan was chartered, with Frank Hoke and Gaston Poole as cofounders. This was the first savings and loan to be organized in Texas since the depression of 1929. Their first office was at 324½ West Jefferson in a real estate office. Mr. Hoke remembers that they rented one half of one table for twenty-five dollars per month to have a place to put their telephone, and records were kept in a plain manila folder on their end of the table. Shortly afterward, however, they rented larger space for a hundred a month, which they subleased. By 1956 they were continuing to grow and were establishing new branches. In 1966 they built a new building at Twelfth and Bishop in Oak Cliff and formed the 8.8 Corporation, acquiring savings and loan associations in various parts of the state. In 1972 Frank Hoke, chairman of the board, and John L. Ingle, president, formed a holding company—the First Texas Financial Corporation—and the assets of the 8.8 Corporation along with the Oak Cliff Savings and Loan assets, were transferred to the holding company. The First Texas Financial Corporation now owns ten associations in Texas, a life insurance company in Arizona, and several casualty insurance agencies. It is the largest savings and loan holding company in Texas, and the Oak Cliff Savings and Loan Association is second largest in Dallas and in 1976 changed its name to First Texas Savings of Dallas.

There are now fifteen strategically located savings and loan institutions in Dallas, some with branches in various parts of the state. The structure has changed somewhat over the years, and they are now involved in making installment and construction loans, as well as long-term mortgage loans. As of December 31, 1975, total savings deposits in Dallas were $1,940,071,383.

INSURANCE

The history of life insurance in Dallas goes back more than seventy-five years. In 1898 a group of farsighted, civic-minded men, which included C. B. Gardner, Louis Blaylock, and George Taylor, met in the Oriental Hotel (the present location of the Baker Hotel) to discuss the founding of what was to become the first life insurance institution to be chartered in Dallas and in the state of Texas. Taking the name "Praetorians" from the elite home guard of the city of Rome, they formed the Modern Order of Praetorians. The foremost thought in the minds of the founders was protection of the home, widows, and orphans through fraternalism and life insurance. At the end of the year, the assets of the company amounted to $49.36, and Louis Blaylock, later to become mayor of Dallas, pledged himself to pay any death claim out of his personal funds until the society had sufficient funds to take care of claims. Their first home office was a three-story building on Main Street near the old Sanger Brothers. Excavation was begun in 1901 for a new building to be located at Main and Stone streets, but due to lack of funds, construction was stopped for several months with a deep hole in the ground. People would stop in the street and laughingly point to the hole where "that skyscraper was to be built," calling it Gardner's Folly. The building was completed in 1908, however, and was the tallest building west of the Mississippi River at that time. Later in 1958 the old fraternal society was converted to a mutual, legal reserve life insurance company and the name changed to the present Praetorian Mutual Life. At the same old location, ground was again broken for a larger and more modern building, and the new seventeen-story Praetorian Building was completed in 1960. The present president is J. N. Harris, Jr.

Another one of the early insurance companies with home offices in Dallas was the present Southwestern Life Insurance Company founded in 1903 with their first office at 310 Main Street. Sam P. Cochran, who also had numerous banking interests, was one of the founders along with E. O. Tenison (a banker, and later first president of the Federal Reserve Bank), Alex Sanger, J. B. Wilson, George W. Jalonick, and W. A. Childress, the first president. In 1912 the Southwestern Life Building was completed at Main and Akard streets during the presidency of T. W. Vardell. During the early 1930s, West Texas was experiencing a severe drought, and T. M. Lucas, who was an important loan officer at that time, had approximately $35 million in ranch and farm loans. Very few were able to repay these loans because of the drought, and so a moratorium was granted on the principal and the interest. However, not a single penny was lost because of the moratorium, and funds later were lent to them for the development of oil wells. Southwestern Life introduced in Dallas the first bank service plan in 1931 which provided for monthly premium payments to be deducted automatically from a policyowner's bank account. In 1961 the territory covered by Southwestern Life was greatly expanded with the acquisition of the Atlantic Life Insurance Company of Richmond, Virginia, and again in 1968 with the acquisition of Universal Life and Accident. In 1964 they moved once again into a new and modern building on the corner of Ross and Akard streets. An extensive reorganization in late 1972 resulted in the formation of a new holding company, the Southwestern Life Corporation, at which time William H. Seay became chairman of the board and president. Today, Southwestern Life is operating in thirty-five states and the District of Columbia, and its combined insurance in force is $8 billion.

By 1908 another one of Dallas' early life insurance companies was chartered. The Southland Life Insurance Company was formed with Colonel John T. Boone as its first president, followed a couple of years later by James A. Stephenson as its president. In 1915 Harry L. Seay became president, and they made the first of many expansions by purchasing the Sam Houston Life Insurance, which was organized in 1909, and the San Antonio Life Insurance Company. Their first home was two rooms on the third floor of a building on Main Street where El Centro College is now located, but by 1918 they had moved into their own home office building next to the Baker Hotel. During the ensuing decades, Southland Life showed rapid growth and added other types of insurance to its programs. In 1953 John W. Carpenter was chairman of the board, Dan C. Williams was president, and Ben H.

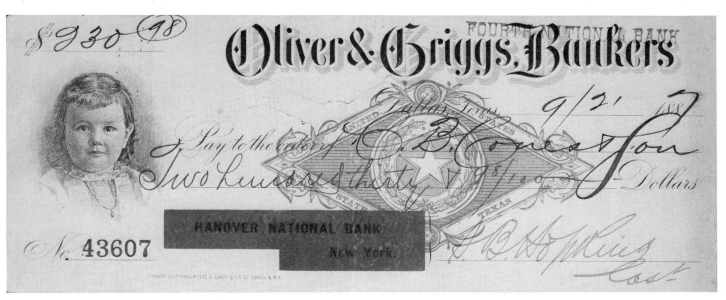

September 21, 1887, check on a Dallas bank for $230.98.

Carpenter was executive vice-president until the death of his father in 1959 when he assumed the post of chairman of the board.

The company continued to grow and in 1959 moved into the Southland Life Tower, a multimillion-dollar forty-two-story building, Dallas' first real skyscraper. The Southland Life Tower is part of the Southland Center, which covers two and a half acres in downtown Dallas and is also the location of the Sheraton-Dallas Hotel. In 1971 changes were made in the corporate structure, and a financial holding company was organized called the Southland Financial Corporation. The management officers of the holding company are Ben H. Carpenter, president and chief executive officer, and Dan C. Williams, chairman of the board. Southland Life at the present time is in forty-five states and the District of Columbia and Puerto Rico, and has insurance in force of $5 billion.

Another of the early insurance companies in Dallas was the Texas Employers' Insurance Association which was formed in 1914 due to the passage by the legislature of the Texas Workmen's Compensation Act, a bill that was sponsored by Senator V. A. Collins, father of Carr P. Collins. The first general manager was Homer W. Mitchell, who was later president and then chairman of the board until his death in 1956. Ben H. Mitchell, his son, joined the association in 1924 as secretary to his father and became president and chairman of the board in 1962. This is the largest company in Dallas writing this kind of insurance. Today it is headed by John F. Stephens, chairman of the board and president.

The United Fidelity Life Insurance Company was founded in 1920 by D. E. Waggoner and his son, D. Easley Waggoner, and started in business at 1025 Elm Street. Today, they are located in one of Dallas' skyscrapers at the same location, with offices in thirty states. M. Cullum Thompson has been president since 1961. In 1970 they became affiliated with Lykes-Youngstown Corporation, which has interests in banking, shipping, basic steel production, and electronics.

In 1927 the Fidelity Union Life Insurance Company was founded by Carr P.

Collins, with their first offices at 1000 Main Street. Their goal for 1964 was set for $1 billion worth of life insurance in force, and they went on to more than triple that amount in the next decade. Because they were a rapidly growing company, they built a new office building in 1953 and later built the adjoining Fidelity Union Tower in 1960. During his career, Carr had many unusual ventures such as Crazy Crystals and the Crazy Hotel at Mineral Wells, Texas. A coast-to-coast radio schedule on NBC promoted the Crazy Water show, with Mary Martin at one time singing on the Crazy Radio programs. Carr has been active all his life in various civic projects, too. Of particular interest to him have been the Baptist Foundation, Baylor Medical Center, and Bishop College.

The Republic National Life was organized in 1937 when Theodore P. Beasley and his associates purchased controlling interest of Republic Life Insurance Company (1930) and merged with it the Public National Life Company at Little Rock, Arkansas, which they also controlled. They are currently doing business in forty-nine states, the District of Columbia, Puerto Rico, and the Virgin Islands, and are among the leaders in the specialized field of reinsurance business. They are also ranked among the fifteen largest in the country when measured by insurance in force.

Dallas is well known for the number of insurance companies with home offices located here which is due, in part, to the passage of the Robertson's Insurance Law in 1907. The Robertson's Law required all life insurance companies doing business in Texas to keep 75 per cent of their legal reserves on Texas policies invested in Texas securities or real estate. This was in addition to the tax levied on gross premium receipts. As a result, many of the out-of-state insurance companies regarded these measures as discriminatory and no longer did business within the state. Ultimately, this stimulated the formation of numerous companies in Texas, and particularly in Dallas. Later, however, many of these out-of-state companies returned to the state and many established their regional headquarters in Dallas.

Today, there are nearly one hundred insurance companies with home offices located in Dallas, and in 1975 the total life insurance written in the state of Texas was $12,466,000,000, or a total of 4.4 per cent of that written in the United States.

THE PRESENT

Until a few years ago, banks, savings and loan institutions, and insurance companies limited their services to taking care of predominantly local needs. Today, this picture has changed significantly. With the restructuring of the financial institutions by means of the holding company, the advent of national bank credit cards, and advanced computer technology, the finance industry has entered a new era.

Many of the banks in Dallas have formed, or become a part of, a bank holding company. The Bank Holding Company Act, which was passed by Congress in 1956

Robert L. Thornton, Jr., was born in Dallas in 1911, only son of the pioneer banker, civic leader, and mayor. He attended Dartmouth College, Southern Methodist University, and Harvard University.

Young Thornton grew up in literally every department of the Mercantile National Bank. During World War II he served in the U. S. Air Force, rose to the rank of lieutenant colonel, and was aide to Major General James Cheney with the first marines to land on Iwo Jima.

Mr. Thornton has been president and board chairman of the Mercantile National Bank and board chairman of the Mercantile Texas Corporation, from which he retired in 1976 to become chairman of the board of Shaw Equipment Company.

Some of his major interests include trusteeship of the Dallas County Community College District and leadership of its foundation, chairmanship of Greater Dallas Crime Commission and Long Range Water Supply Commission. He is one of the three state commissioners of the Texas Alcoholic Beverage Commission and is also a trustee of Southwestern Medical Foundation and a director of the State Fair of Texas, the University of Texas at Arlington Development Board, Mercantile National Bank, Wrather Corporation, and Greater Dallas Planning Council.

The late Mrs. Thornton was the former Miss Temple Webb.

and later amended in 1966 and 1970, defines a bank holding company as any company (a) that owns, controls, or holds with power to vote 25 per cent or more of the voting shares of one or more banks, or (b) that controls in any manner the election of a majority of the directors of one or more banks, or (c) the Federal Reserve Board determines that the company directly or indirectly exercises a controlling influence over the management of policies of the bank. Since all bank holding companies are under the jurisdiction of the Federal Reserve Board, their approval must be obtained to become a holding company.

An important change taking place in the nation's banking structure in the past thirty years has been the dramatic increase in branch banking from four thousand branch offices in 1945 to thirty thousand in 1975. Because the state of Texas prohibits branch banking, the holding company permits growth far beyond that which would be possible in a single bank. Such growth is important to meet the financial needs of the primary, or larger, customers, and without the business of these large corporate customers, local banks could not fully develop their peripheral services such as trust and international departments. Many of the insurance companies and savings and loan institutions have likewise found it to their advantage to form holding companies and take on new roles. This is exemplified by the recent statement of James B. Goodson, president of the Southland Life Insurance Company: "Traditionally, life insurance companies have been providers of financing rather than users, but as they change and become part of holding company complexes, depending upon the type of business the holding companies engage in, the new present entity will likely be a borrower, particularly if they are involved in heavy capital use businesses, such as real estate development." Some of the advantages of the holding company structure for insurance companies lies in their greater freedom to make acquisitions, and thus to expand into new geographical areas, and a greater flexibility for investments.

A few years ago the banks also entered into the credit card business. The Texas Bank and Trust Company was the first in Dallas to issue a bank credit card which was known as the "Charge-It Card." This was followed later by the "Presto-Charge," which was issued by the Preston State Bank. These early cards were used by local customers at the stores of local merchants. Now, however, the various bank cards have been consolidated primarily into two national systems: the BankAmericard, issued in Dallas only by the Texas Bank and Trust Company, and the Master Charge card, issued locally by several Dallas banks. These cards are used nationally and internationally for a wide range of services.

At this time the banks and savings and loans are beset with many sweeping technological changes brought about by the computer. Some time during the 1960s the Federal Reserve Board enforced the usage of magnetic ink-coded checks because they could be processed more rapidly by the computer. Then in the 1970s the major bank credit card systems began accepting electronic rather than paper records from their respective centers, in addition to electronic credit authorization. Today both institutions have electronic tellers for depositing and cashing checks and they are in competition for direct payroll deposits. All financial organizations have become vitally interested in these new electronic developments, and Lloyd S. Bowles, Sr., chairman of the board of Dallas Federal Savings and Loan Association, recently commented, "Present developments with electronic terminals in retail outlets are occurring nationwide on an experimental basis, and the present national acceptance under the limited approach and continued support from the technological side suggests a widespread use, barring congressional restrictions."

Today the "Dallas spirit" is serving the healthy, growing economy of the Southwest with many national and international industries establishing their corporate or regional headquarters in the Dallas area. Trade and convention centers have been built to keep abreast of our expanding markets (just as our oversized airport can accommodate the new Concorde airplane), and the sizable growth of our holding companies, together with the advent of computerization and world-wide trade, calls for international branches or service units. As a result of this business expansion, the financial institutions in Dallas continue to grow in size and to expand their services to the individual and the corporate customer, not only locally, but nationally and internationally.

Dallas thinks big. It always has. It continues to do so.

WHERE WE ARE GOING

To me, the transformation of Dallas into one of the fastest growing metropolitan areas of the country reflects long-range planning and the aggressiveness and creativity of its business and civic leaders. Its progress still does not depend on mere chance or location. Determined to rank Dallas among the leading cities in the country, the financial leaders have used their time and talents, and their financing, to make Dallas a dynamic, growing city.

Let us evaluate some of the factors that have enabled Dallas to rise to its present position of leadership in the Southwest. In its early history, Dallas bankers helped to finance the wheat and cotton industry. Later they were among the first in the country to lend money on underground oil reserves; today they help to finance world-wide ventures such as the North Sea oil explorations. After World War II, the city's banks helped to finance many of the city's growing industrial firms such as Texas Instruments, which is now an international company with plants in over fifteen nations, and the Southland Corporation, which has over 5,400 7-Eleven convenience stores in the United States and four foreign countries. In addition, banks in co-operation with other financial institutions have helped to establish many new companies in the city. Fifty years ago Dallas businessmen actively campaigned together to locate the Federal Reserve Bank in Dallas because it would be "good for the city"; today, they work together just as hard for the future of Dallas by building the largest airport in the world, the 20,000-acre Dallas–Fort Worth Airport, thereby increasing the importance of Dallas as a national and international trade center.

Important to Dallas' growth has been its international outlook. The economies of the Southwest, of Texas, and of Dallas have a long history of exporting to world markets. Years ago when Dallas was a leading wheat and cotton market, it had the banking and commercial expertise to serve the requirements of international trade in competition with coastal cities. Cotton men settled in Dallas from all over the world—from England, Italy, France, Japan, and many other countries. Dallas business leaders have vigorously charted an international course in both trade and investments. Today, two of our large commercial banks place twenty-first and twenty-second in size in the nation and are aggressively expanding their international departments. As Robert H. Stewart III, chairman of the board of First International Bancshares (the largest bank holding company in Texas) remarked recently, "We grew because our customers grew; their operations went world-wide, and so we opened international branches in many parts of the world."

Another new challenge for our financial institutions lies ahead in the coming decade. The banking transactions of every individual from every walk of life may soon be changed by electronics. Payrolls may soon be credited directly into each individual's bank by means of magnetic tape sent to automated clearinghouses. The U. S. Air Force started crediting their payrolls in this manner in 1975, and the U. S.

Treasury, the largest single issuer of checks, began making some of their social security payments to their recipients electronically in 1976 in lieu of checks. In the future, deposits and withdrawals could be made at electronic terminals in retail outlets which are connected to your local bank, and payment of regular monthly bills such as insurance premiums, installment loans, and mortgage payments could all be paid by your banks electronically—making trips to the bank and the writing of many checks unnecessary!

The electronic funds transfer system, a paperless payments system, has already begun in California and other parts of the United States, and will undoubtedly affect all banks and savings and loans in the country, as well as the Dallas area, at some point in the future. In Dallas, the Southwestern Automated Clearing House (SWACH), a nonprofit organization serving the entire Eleventh Federal Reserve District, expects to be operational in the spring of 1976 and will begin to handle direct payroll deposits. The Federal Reserve Bank in Dallas has agreed to operate the SWACH by producing the facilities, computer hardware, and personnel and will be responsible for the distribution of electronic items. Primarily, the automated clearinghouses have been formed to reduce the huge volume of checks being processed and also to help the consumer eliminate some of the paper work involved. Speaking on this subject, Jimmie Aston, chairman of the board of the Republic of Texas Corporation, said, "The current environment today, when we are on the threshold of electronic transfer technology, is vastly different than when Texas banks and banking had their beginnings. The development of electronic transfer and communications technology is certain to produce dramatic changes, not only in the banking industry as we have known it, but also other sectors of the financial system." In the meantime, all financial and nonfinancial competitors stand ready to explore the opportunities that electronic transfer technology will present to their customers.

As they grew in size, our banks, savings and loan institutions, and insurance companies began to enlarge their quarters or build new buildings. In 1889 the business district of Dallas was bounded by Murphy, Elm, Lamar, and Commerce streets—a seven-block area. Lamar Street was known as the Wall Street of Dallas because so many of the early banks were located there, or within a block of it. The role and function of the Central Business District still contains the largest single concentration of financial activities including the Federal Reserve. Most of the large commercial banks and insurance companies find it to their advantage to be part of concentrated activity within the central area, and although they have built newer and larger buildings, they have stayed within a few blocks of their original offices. Some of the skyscrapers built by banks and insurance companies are the Southland Center, Republic National Bank Building and Tower, Southwestern Life Building, Fidelity Union Tower, First National Bank Building, First International Building, the LTV Building, Praetorian Building, United Fidelity Building, and the Mercantile Buildings. This pattern has not been true, however, with many savings and loan institutions. Because their main interests have revolved around the consumer rather than commercial customers, some have started moving their main head-quarters into the suburban areas, with branches in the downtown area.

The most extensive real estate project—Main Place—although built by the Overton and Murchison families, was catalyzed by the Texas Bank and Trust Company, which has made its home there. One Main Place, a thirty-two-story, two-million-square-foot building, is the first phase of a ten-acre tract in the "Wall Street" area of Dallas.

It is probably one of the most significant center city developments in our nation—certainly the most important urban project Dallas has known—for a number of reasons. In an attempt to get to the root causes of urban decay, it employed several important concepts:

- It encouraged the various governmental authorities to develop the circumferential freeway system around the downtown area, thereby eliminating "through traffic" from downtown vehicular congestion.

- It separated, in the design of Main Place, conflicting forms of traffic so that trucks, people, and automobiles could navigate on separate levels with minimal interference.

- An attempt was made to establish the "two-shift" city by extending the life of downtown beyond the usual 6 P.M. closing. An extensive retail area—with pedestrian mall, fountain, and landscaping—featuring restaurants and clubs was installed in One Main Place.

- In an age when government assumes an increasingly dominant role, this ten-acre tract was assembled by private enterprise parcel by parcel (ninety in all requiring four-hundred signatures) over a thirty-year period (1936 to 1964). This became undoubtedly the largest parcel-by-parcel assemblage of downtown property in modern times. More significant is that while One Main Place has made a fine beginning, the fact of this single ownership ensures the completion of the Main Place development.

Main Place has influenced many places—including Johannesburg, South Africa, where a downtown project was modeled after it. But nowhere has it had greater effect than in Dallas where the city has adopted its concepts as its official development plan. Under construction, at this writing, is a pedestrian-trucking network that joins the Republic National Bank Building, First National Bank, First International Building, Metropolitan Savings and Loan Association, and Texas Bank and Trust at One Main Place, and Holiday Inn, Loews Theater and Garage, with Thanksgiving Square as the connector. The Mercantile Buildings, which one day will be a part of this network, has in fact developed its own pedestrian concourse within its buildings.

Since the early beginnings of Dallas, the financial leaders have continued playing the dual role of businessman and civic leader. Though fiercely competitive in business, they are just as determined and enthusiastic in their support of civic and cultural affairs and join together as patrons of the arts, school board members, city planners, fund raisers, and philanthropists. Some have given land to the city for public parks such as Tenison Park and Thanksgiving Square, while others have given vast amounts of money to hospitals and colleges or formed foundations for research, charities, and the arts. The banks in the Dallas Clearing House have contributed millions of dollars through the years to various charities and cultural institutions, and the Dallas County Screening Committee, a voluntary organization composed of representatives of twenty-four business and professional groups and associations, raised a sum of over $20 million in 1974 alone for fund-raising projects. Recognizing the need for the involvement and support of young leaders to continue these programs and projects, a new program called Leadership Dallas has been initiated through the Chamber of Commerce to involve these younger members in shaping the future growth of Dallas.

Nobody can say with certainty what the future will bring. Yet one thing has remained constant—the strong desire for high achievement that has characterized Dallas from the beginning. This is what we "bank on" for the future.*

* The author wishes to thank the Dallas Clearing House for their assistance in the research for this chapter.

THE LOOK OF DALLAS

Some landmarks. Dallas' buildings are a varied blend of designs and periods, from the statue opposite on the old Administration Building of the State Fair, believed to have been the original Dallas Coliseum, to One Main Place (*page 131*), from the Old Red Courthouse (*page 131*) to the UCC Tower (*page 133, top row, left*), from the 1920s elegance of the old Majestic Theater (*page 132*) to the Frank Lloyd Wright-designed Kalita Humphreys Theater (*page 133, fifth row, left*). It is a city of skyscrapers and neon, of the delicacy of a gazebo in City Park (*page 134*) and the solidity of Old City Hall (*page 135*), and of many touches of its past, as in the Millermore Mansion (*page 134*) in City Park, built originally in Oak Cliff by a contemporary of John Neely Bryan's.

Rabbi Emeritus of Temple Emanu-El, Dr. Levi A. Olan came to Dallas in 1949 from Rochester, New York; Cincinnati, Ohio; and Worcester, Massachusetts. He is visiting professor at Texas Christian University, Fort Worth, and visiting lecturer at Perkins School of Theology, Southern Methodist University. He has also served as visiting professor at the University of Texas at both Austin and Arlington, Emory University in Atlanta, Institute of Religion and Human Development in Houston, and Leo Baeck College in London. Dr. Olan was on the board of regents of the University of Texas and is the author of books and monographs in religious scholarship and philosophy. He has contributed himself vigorously to every humanitarian cause in Dallas for over two decades.

Religion

by DR. LEVI A. OLAN

The churches in Dallas believe in Christian charity and are against social change.

There is loud preaching against liquor, pari-mutuel betting, and pornography. But the social message is not heard from the pulpits of the city, and this in the face of some desperate social exigencies—like poverty, unemployment, racism, and civil rights.

And thus, religion in Dallas is like religion in any large American city—only more so. Here, religion is big. And, institutionally, it possesses a most unhumble penchant for desiring to be *first*.

An anecdote captures the high place religion occupies in the estimation of the city leaders. A meeting of a small group of community workers met in the board room of one of the largest city banks, a not uncommon event. The president of the bank presided and opened the meeting in native style. He announced that Dallas is the seat of the four largest churches of their denominations in the world: Baptist, Methodist, Presbyterian, and Christian. The Rabbi present looked uncomfortable. The chairman asked whether Temple Emanu-El is the largest in the world, to which the reply was "No! But we have the largest mortgage in the world!"

Part of the accent on bigness may be written off because of the natural tendency of Texans to brag. Yet even after this discount has been made, there is much left in its popular appellation, Big D. It demonstrates an insatiable craving for *big* banks, *big* football, and *big* religion. It is the home of 750,000 Protestants, 90,000 Catholics, and 22,000 Jews—functioning through more than twelve hundred churches and synagogues.

OVERLEAF: Sacred Heart Cathedral.

The Baptists constitute the largest religious denomination, with Methodists and Catholics in second and third place. Popular local legend tells of a stranger who asks a Dallasite whether the "Back to God Crusade" has reached the city. The firm reply he got was "I didn't know it left."

A tourist ride through the city discloses not only its many churches but also the hundred institutions and agencies sponsored by the religious community. Four of the largest and highly accredited hospitals are sponsored by the Baptist, Methodist, Catholic, and Presbyterian churches. Three of the largest universities were established by the Methodist, Catholic, and Baptist governing bodies. There are in addition a number of secondary schools maintained by Catholic, Episcopalian, and Jewish congregations. If one adds to these the welfare agencies under denominational sponsorship, the result is impressive. Those who are prone to measure in monetary terms estimate the property value of religion in Dallas to be about a quarter of a billion dollars. In the words of a prominent Dallas layman, "Religion in Dallas is big business."

It was, however, not always thus, for the beginnings were starkly humble. In the 1840s when the white man first came to explore the area there was no definite place to meet for worship except a brush arbor or a clearing in the woods. Tiny mud-plastered cabins soon appeared to serve as "Sunday meeting" houses. By the year 1875 their churches were described as "little, humble frame buildings, wanting in beauty, in paint, in comfort, and having but one thing in abundance—and that was religion." The old courthouse, which during the week sheltered a share of criminals, became on Sunday a meeting place for Christian services. The general store and the livery stable were transformed once a week for religious worship. One hearty band of faithful believers met in the saloon, after the bottles were cleaned out. If a building was not available, they joined in prayer out of doors.

The growth of religion in Dallas is rich with exciting drama. Its rudimentary beginnings occurred while Indians were the ever present enemy. Worshipers carried their guns to church prepared to meet attack before and after services. One of the earliest worship gatherings met in the little cabin of John Neely Bryan, with whose appearance in the area the city of Dallas designates its beginning. There was a Methodist Conference in Dallas in 1847, the records of which disclose an expenditure of $4.95, $.43 of which was paid for quartering moderator Biggs. In the spring of 1844 Thomas Brown, a visiting minister, preached a sermon in the home of W. M. Cochran situated in the northern part of the settlement. The Cochran Chapel stands today on the site of that home, where the first deeded and dedicated church property in Dallas County was established.

The denominational expansion followed swiftly. The Baptists, today the largest group, held their first worship service in 1846 and organized their first congregation in 1857. A second was started in 1863 which later moved to Pleasant View where it continues its program today. It is the oldest Baptist church in Dallas County.

In 1857 an Episcopal priest, George Rottenstein, came to the city and founded

OVERLEAF: A religious revival at the Cotton Bowl.

St. Matthew's Church, which in 1875 was declared the Cathedral of the New Missionary District. Bishop Garrett, who so declared it, was what we loosely today describe as a charismatic figure. On February 5, 1875, he announced: "I have adopted Dallas as my See city, St. Matthew's Church therein as my cathedral, and in the name of our God here have I set up my banner and grounded my staff, that the enemy may not prevail." The cathedral stood across from the Santa Fe Railroad Station. The train that arrived on Sunday at noon inspired this description: "As the minister was beginning to wax eloquent upon the attractions of the New Jerusalem, hissing steam and energetic efforts of hotel runners and hack drivers loaded the air with common things of the earth in a most distressing manner." The cathedral soon moved to the campus of St. Mary's College, where it stands today.

The Roman Catholic Church was formally established in Dallas in 1869 when Father Joseph Martiniere arrived in the small village to found a very small parish he called Sacred Heart. Before the turn of the century it moved "out in the country," which is its present site, and which was dedicated as the cathedral seat of the diocese in 1902.

Dan G. Malloy, a Scotch-Irishman, rode into town in 1850 and announced that he had just been ordained a minister in the Cumberland Presbyterian Church and that he was ready to begin saving souls. He preached his first sermon in the now historic John Neely Bryan cabin. Later his congregation, in fair weather, gathered for worship on the banks of the Trinity River. This was the forerunner of the present downtown City Temple Presbyterian Church U.S.A., which observes the year 1850 as the date of its origin.

The first worship service of the Christian church was conducted in 1857 in a very small hut between Market and Lamar streets, where a marker informs us there stood the first Protestant church building within the city limits of Dallas. Out of this there grew the Central Christian Church, which is now housed in impressive quarters on fashionable West Side Drive.

The "newest" of the large congregations to establish itself in Dallas is the Lutheran, which followed settlers of German and Scandinavian origin to their new land. A Missouri Synod service was conducted somewhere in the downtown area in 1874 and was the predecessor of the Zion Lutheran Church, which is now located on historic Swiss Avenue.

Historically, a Jewish community begins by acquiring a place to bury its dead and creating a benevolent society to provide for the poor. The handful of Jews who dared to travel as far as Dallas, Texas, when it was first opened up, followed the traditional pattern. In 1871 a dozen men met in the lodge hall of the B'nai Brith over Sanger Brothers department store. After they had cared for the dead and the poor, they began making plans to provide for their religious needs. They adopted "Temple Emanu-El" as the name of their congregation and built its first sanctuary on Commerce Street. After two moves to larger quarters they built the present building in 1957, which is often described as one of the finest examples of modern religious architecture, where it serves about 2,200 families who are associated with Reform Judaism. A Conservative Jewish congregation began in 1884 when three Jews met in Wasserman's store on Elm Street to found a synagogue that would provide a religious program traditional in nature. This has grown into a large congregation, Shearith Israel, numbering 1,200 families and housed in a beautiful building. A third congregation, Orthodox in its affiliation, Tifereth Israel, began in 1890 and today serves 375 families in a new impressive building. These congregations were located originally in South Dallas and followed their members to North Dallas. The most recent Jewish congregation, Temple Shalom, began about ten years ago and now serves almost five hundred members in a modern building. It is affiliated with the Reform Jewish movement.

The city of Dallas has never experienced a static period, and its religious community has not only kept pace with its spectacular growth, it has surpassed it. Upon the early, rugged foundations built by the pioneers of faith there has been built a religious community often designated as the religious capital of the world. The spectrum of denominational allegiance runs from the exuberant pentecostal to the rationalistic Unitarian. It includes Black Muslims, Mormons, Bahai, Adventists, Greek Orthodox, a church for the gay people, and a Christian Jewish congregation. It is the home of almost every religious expression found in America. Many churches are wholly independent of any denominational body.

If variety is the spice of life, Dallas is religiously a very spicy town. Large revival meetings periodically contribute to the religious life of the city. They arrive with tents and colorful revivalist preachers as headliners. In 1886 Dwight Moody and his partner, Sankey, held revival meetings in the old Iron Building, better known as the Skating Rink. Each meeting was attended by four thousand people, and the press reported that "the evangelist blazed a way to salvation that many joyfully followed." Moody's standing with the business community is best described by the order of a rich merchant to his clerk: "Make out a check for Mr. Moody for whatever amount he requests."

Evangelists came regularly and drew large crowds. The Reverend George R. Stuart is reported to have "convulsed his audience with his humorous recitals." In 1912 Gypsy Smith brought out 16,000; Billy Sunday in 1916 packed them in; and in 1953 Billy Graham filled the Cotton Bowl Football Stadium with 75,504 admiring followers. The only revival preacher to whom the Dallas community was cool, even frigid, was the Reverend Henry Ward Beecher, whose abolitionist sentiments were too strong for their proslavery sympathies. So they come and they go with or without tents, men, and women—preachers of the Word of God. Their arrivals and departures are announced in large newspaper advertisements as well as on television and radio.

Dallasites often attribute the phenomenal growth of their city to a few dynamic leaders, since the area is without natural resources. Its religious expansion received much impetus from several brilliant clergymen whose years of service ran concur-

rently with its lively civic progress. The Reverend Dr. George Truett, admiringly called Prince of Preachers, served the First Baptist Church from 1897 to 1944. His radio sermons are rebroadcast today as examples of powerful religious preaching.

Rabbi David Lefkowitz assumed the leadership of Temple Emanu-El in 1920 and served it until he died in 1955. His humane and universal messages reached beyond his congregation and his city. His voice through radio was known in every village and town of North Texas.

Bishop Joseph Patrick Lynch arrived in Dallas in 1900 to serve a very small community of Catholics. When he died in 1954, they constituted the third largest religious group in the city.

These three religious leaders, Protestant, Jew, and Catholic, were instrumental in creating a religious climate favorable to the dynamism of the vigorous commercial expansion. They illustrated a truth that the world is just beginning to learn—one can be loyal to his particular faith while serving the human needs of all peoples. There was ecumenism here long before that word became popular. Dallas was built by uniquely gifted leaders both civic and religious.

Religion in America is two-dimensional—civil and salvational.

Civil religion celebrates the "American Way of Life." It asserts that religion is necessary to the health of the nation. Justice William O. Douglas, in a Supreme Court decision, said: "We are a religious people whose institutions presuppose a Supreme Being." He is, at the same time, a strict separationist on the issue of Church and State.

"Our government," said President Eisenhower, "makes no sense unless it is founded in a deeply felt religious faith, and I don't care what it is."

America is God-oriented, not ecclesiastical.

It is natural to stamp "In God We Trust" on our coins and to salute the flag with "one nation under God."

A modern poet has sung:

> God is very big in Dallas,
>
> Just about everybody talks about God.
>
> I don't think you could ever amount to much in Dallas,
>
> If you went around bad-mouthing God.

Church membership is an unwritten requirement for anyone seeking political office or some other position of stature. A young successful businessman was selected by his peers to be honored as the Young Businessman of the Year, only to be informed that they must regrettably withdraw the honor since he was not a member of any church or synagogue. He joined one instantly and was happily chosen and joyfully honored.

The Reverend Norman Vincent Peale is probably the most articulate spokesman for civil religion in America, and he is the favorite preacher of the Dallas business community. He addressed the largest religious gathering in the history of the city at the State Fair of Texas, and he said: "We need people who believe so in God and in the United States that they will witness to the greatness of both, wherever they go. The U.S.A. is a lovely land . . . don't run it down. Talk it up, pray it up. Make it, what by the grace of God, it can be." Civil religion in Dallas reflects its cultural climate. It is an essential ingredient in the success formula of Big D.

The cynic will lift his eyebrow and sneeringly talk about wrapping oneself in the holy flag. Questioning the purity of religious language and observance is a very old tradition, harking back to the Hebrew prophets and to Jesus. There is often much for the doubter to question. Civil religion, however, does contribute significantly to the well-being of the city.

In 1950 the Greater Dallas Council of Churches was organized, and today it represents over two hundred churches of different denominations. It is a united effort by the Christian community to do important religious work in the city. Current active programs are involved in housing, support of public schools, chaplaincy in hospitals and prisons, and a counseling center for troubled people. All of its work is a positive expression of religious concern in a united way. The leadership of the Chamber of Commerce often assumes leadership of the Council of Churches. The religious leaders of the city have not, as yet, explored the rich resources of civil religion toward ameliorating some of the severe social imbalances that affect Dallas.

Religion in Dallas reflects the conservatism of the community at large. The social gospel as expressed by the National Council of Churches in America is not acceptable to the lay leadership of the local churches.

Salvational religion runs concurrently with civil religion. Its primary concern is the redemption of the individual from sin, for which each church has its own program. The dividing factor among them is theology, or more specifically, revelation. The fundamentalist or conservative churches guide their people by a literal interpretation of the biblical word. The more liberal churches teach the Bible as a divinely inspired book but not literally God's word. The former accept the miracles as true, the latter speak of them as myth.

Dallas' religious life is largely conservative, and there is a vigorous growing movement toward more of it. The late Richard Niebuhr spoke of "the accommodation of religion to the caste system of society." Some Dallas churches save the souls of the affluent, others of the middle class, and still others of the poor.

The cynic, again, will cock his eye and mock: "Does God know the difference?" Yet he misses the positive role this class separation plays in the life of the people. Ask a Dallasite his religion, and he will give you in response the name of the church he attends. What he is expressing is a sense of identity which is comfortable and satisfying.

Dallas churches and synagogues are busy places: they serve more food than all the restaurants put together. Their people eat together, sing, study, and pray together; and, in many churches, they play and dance together. The church in Dallas is a community, a fellowship in a world growing increasingly impersonal and lonely.

Ethnically Dallas is white, black, brown, and red. The minority groups have, in recent years, become active in their pursuit of civil rights and liberties, but never militant. Religiously, there is almost no effort made to integrate them, nor do they seem to desire it.

The churches of the Mexican-Americans and American Indians are salvational only; the blacks share in the civil religion of the city. Their pastors have their own "Ministerial Alliance," but many of them are members of the Pastors Association, in which one of them was recently elected president. The black churches are members of the Greater Dallas Council of Churches and their leaders play an active role in its program. A black clergyman has been a superintendent of the Methodist churches of the city.

There is an inner class structure within the black religious community not unlike that in the white. Their main-line churches are led by clergymen who have received theological education in a seminary. Many of their members belong to the NAACP and share in some of the efforts to achieve better conditions for the blacks in the city. They carefully separate themselves, however, from those who take to militant protest. Indeed, they were lukewarm to Martin Luther King, Jr., when he visited the city. Their contacts with white leaders in the civil religious program of the city have not advanced the integration of the schools. It does, however, allow a black clergyman to secure a favor for one of his members in jobs, schools, and welfare. This enables the leaders of the city to have a guiding word in the black community. As in white religious life, many black churches are wholly salvational, parochial, taking no part in civil religion. Many of these are pentecostal, and all are theologically conservative.

The latest development in the religious life of America is the rapid growth of pentecostal or charismatic forms of worship. Dallas is not only keeping pace with the nation, it is leading them all. Essentially this represents an effort to free the spirit from rigid forms. The worshiper seeks direct communion with the Holy Spirit, something beyond the Word itself. In fact, glossalia is an integral part of charismatic religion, the speaking in tongues, an endeavor to get beyond the rational to the real.

There have always been pentecostal churches, both white and black, from the Holy Roller type to the more restrained Assembly of God. The surprisingly new development is the spread of this charismatic religion to the main-line churches—to the Catholic, Episcopalian, Methodist, Baptist, and others. It is fast becoming as strong among the more affluent as among the poor, and finds adherents among both clergymen and laity.

Any interpretation of this trend is a subject for the sociologist and psychologist. There is probably some relationship of this latest religious trend to the radical changes that are shaking our social, economic, and political life today. The uncer-

tainty of morals and manners, the search for authority and identity, the need to experience God, not just to read about Him, is the most vital religious expression in Dallas at the moment.

Dallas is a city very conscious of its image. It aspires to the role of a great and dynamic metropolis. Religion is an integral part of the image, and the city takes pride in the meetings in Dallas of eight national and international bodies in one year. The largest evangelical crusade ever attempted in America, Key 73, attracting 250,000 followers, gathered in Dallas. The business community enthusiastically helped promote this stupendous, dramatic religious event—both with money and with spirit.

It is common for visitors to the city to exclaim in wonder at the intense construction program going on now. Recently, a prominent national religious leader, after a tour of the city, commented, "Dallas is the only city in America where they still build new churches."

And now, the supreme religious talisman is built right in the middle of the business district. On a whole block of land surrounded by towering bank structures of steel and stone, Thanksgiving Square is a reality with grass, shrubs, and water to create a green oasis in a cement land.

The unique and distinguishing feature is a chapel designed by one of America's leading architects where citizens of all faiths may be reminded that "it is good to give thanks unto the Lord."

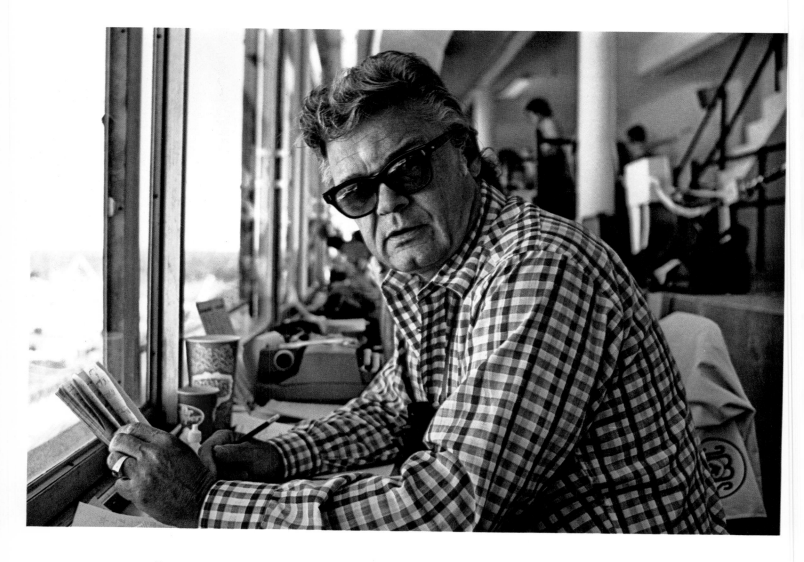

Executive Sports Editor William Forrest (Blackie) Sherrod has had every possible honor and award nationally, regionally, and locally as outstanding sportswriter. He has been with the Dallas *Times Herald* since 1958 and is a member of the board of directors.

Born in Belton, Texas, in 1923, and a graduate of Howard Payne College, he served in the U. S. Navy Air Corps as torpedo plane gunner and received three decorations.

Prior to his association with the Dallas *Times Herald,* he was with the Fort Worth *Press.* He is coauthor of the books *Darrell Royal Talks Football* (Englewood Cliffs: Prentice-Hall, 1963) and *Play to Win* (Boston: Little, Brown, 1971). A collection of his newspaper columns, *Scattershooting,* has also been published and many appear in the past eighteen editions of the annual *Best Sports Stories,* published by E. P. Dutton.

Mr. Sherrod has served as president of both the Football Writers Association of America and the Texas Sportswriters Association.

Sports

by BLACKIE SHERROD

Historians will probably pull thoughtfully on their old briars, tug intellectually on ear lobes, and decree that the sports story of Dallas be divided into phases. Eras and such. As if all history ain't.

There first were the celluloid collar days, the whiskery gatherings at Fair Park to watch baseball at Gaston Park there and see the horses and trotters run foot races at the park track and gaze respectfully as Harry Greb punched on Johnny Celmars. And later, this particular era would follow baseball over to Joe Gardner Park on the Trinity cliffs, kids hooking streetcars across the river to stare worshipfully at the likes of Snipe Conley and Slim Love, swathed cruelly in heavy flannel uniforms with impressive collections of tobacco stains. These were days before air conditioning aggravated the sinuses of the earth, and the ball yard was a pleasant place to relax, especially after the event of night baseball in 1932.

Then there was the Cotton Bowl stage, when the big concrete saucer was poured in 1932, a marvel of its time.

Of course, there was the Rose Bowl era of Southern Methodist University in the mid-thirties. Mind you, this was a time when Dallas was still a rather provincial town, united behind the local university, the local baseball team, the local whatever. An alumnus of the University of Iowa, say, or Cornell was eyed suspiciously, as if he were a card-carrying something or other. Even the Texas A&M exes and the University of Texas grads met privately and spoke when spoken to. The Dallas football fan, by and large, was an SMU fan. And, say, did any other Southwest team ever play in the Rose Bowl? Not on your tinnytype, they didn't. None but the 1935 SMU bunch.

The birth of the Cotton Bowl game itself, brain child of an inventive promoter named Curtis Sanford, was a noteworthy phase in city history.

Then there came the Doak Walker era, the single most electric personality in Dallas athletic history, the little flat-faced gridder of SMU in the immediate post-World War II days. That period, also, saw the rebirth of minor league baseball interest, the salad days of the old Texas League when citizens finally fought off the wartime grimness and lined up to spend their savings and enjoy themselves again without feeling guilty.

Next was the Dallas Cowboy–Dallas Texan era, when pro football returned, and after some lean, angry days, stayed to establish itself and prosper. And then finally, the Texas Ranger period, when major league baseball arrived in these parts and clawed for survival as a sprout on a rocky cliff, then caught and rooted and grew tall.

Scattered among these major sports monuments were minor stages, not all of them happy. There was the first abortive try at professional football, an embarrassing spasm in 1952. There was the gradual growth of a major golf tournament for the city. There was the failure of major league basketball, the collapse of a big-time auto racing project, the depressing decline of SMU interest, and the patient struggle of soccer.

Through the modern sports history of the city, Dallas has become known as a city that "only supports a winner." And in a broad sense, this is true. But it doesn't make the town a leper colony. There are many cities within the nation with the same birthmark. It concerns the city's economic make-up.

Mostly, sports are best supported at the turnstiles in industrial areas, in Detroit, in Pittsburgh, in Chicago, where the factories belch smoke and the worker has a lamp on his cap or grease on his hands and a thirst for diversion as well as a thirst for other pleasures. This goes back to the tenement days, when the honest laborer came home to shed his shirt and sit on the fire escape with a mug of beer and meditate on the unholy misery of the working class. This guy went, and goes, to the ball park to work off his frustrations, or maybe just to escape the self-styled drudgery of his existence. He needs heroes and he needs villains.

Mostly, a half century ago, he understood baseball, for he grew up with that sport. Now he understands football and, in the violent spirit of the times, prefers the crunching collisions over the artistic double play.

Now this guy goes to the park or the stadium regardless of his team's fortunes. If his guys are winning, he goes to yell his approval. If they are losing, he goes to bleat his derision. Get the bum outta there. Hey, Bronk, you got iron for brains? Move around, Moose, you're killing the grass. Put your mask back on, ump, you're scaring the children.

Philadelphia is like this, even now. When the football Eagles were sore and downtrodden, as has been their custom, still there are sell-out crowds. But they are anti-crowds. They came to boo poor Joe Kuharich, the coach. Heck, they even booed Sonny Jurgensen, the season he was winning the league passing title.

Bob Uecker, the old Phillies catcher, tells about the time the ballplayers' children had an Easter egg hunt and fans showed up to boo the kids who didn't find any eggs.

"When the game is rained out, they go to the airport and boo landings," says Uecker.

This is a definite fan-type, the customer in industrial centers. He actually is the backbone of sports economy in this country.

Once, when the Cowboys were a half-dozen years old, they were playing someone in the Cotton Bowl and gave the distinct impression their shoestrings were tied together. As the squad drearily left the field at halftime, they were followed by a resounding *braaacccck* of jeers from the once-loyal assembly.

"Pro football," club president Tex Schramm said happily, "has arrived in Dallas."

But this is not necessarily so.

Dallas has little very heavy industry. It has insurance suites instead of hearths, computers instead of assembly lines, banks instead of foundries, fashions instead of forges. The Dallas guy doesn't seem to crave this outlet. He doesn't grit his teeth in frustration. He is more inclined to shrug.

Now, if his team is winning, fine and dandy. He enjoys the winning atmosphere. He associates with it. He relates.

But if his team is losing, well, he somehow feels embarrassed. To cover the embarrassment, the feeling of inferiority, he doesn't go to the park and throw beer bottles. He shrugs and stays at home, or goes to a movie or a lake. He feels himself too blasé to rant and rave and call down wrath of the heavens on Tom Landry or Frank Lucchesi. Oh, there have been boo-birds spotted in these parts, hooting at Don Meredith or Jeff Burroughs, but theirs is not a dominant sect, not nearly like the raucous critics of other climes. Heck, once at a Washington Redskin game in Kennedy Stadium in December, the crowd booed Santa Claus.

But the Dallasite is more apt to take it personally. Example: when the Washington Senators moved to Arlington Stadium, the team was overcome with modesty and so was the attendance. The Rangers were butts for all baseball jokes. Some cynics called it the worst baseball team ever assembled. There was only one player anybody had ever heard of before, Frank Howard, and he was far past his prime. The Rangers finished far, far in the basement for their first two seasons, and their attendance failed to reach 700,000. This was considered most disappointing for a new territory just being exposed to major league baseball. And most of that attendance, surveys showed, came from Tarrant County and the Mid-Cities area, little from Dallas itself.

Came 1974 and suddenly the Rangers became respectable. Young players like Jeff Burroughs and Toby Harrah and Mike Hargrove and Lenny Randle and Jim Sundberg became of age as performers, as they were always destined to do someday. An old-timer, Ferguson Jenkins, came in a trade and pitched magnificently. The Rangers jumped into contention for the American League west division and stayed within swinging distance of Oakland throughout the season, finally finishing second. It was one of the most drastic turn-arounds in baseball history. And the attendance shot up to 1,153,902, fourth highest in the twelve-team American League. From second lowest to fourth highest in one short year.

Reason: the Dallas spectator was no longer embarrassed by his team's performance. His team was not getting beat 15–1. His outfielders were no longer running into each other; his base runners were no longer stumbling over sacks.

The Dallas Cowboys went through the same experience. In the early days, before the team became a serious contender, there were enough empty seats for an Elvis Presley concert. But once the team became something other than the league patsy, the customers came.

In that respect, perhaps Dallas can be justifiably described as a city that supports only a winner. But so can San Diego and Atlanta and Houston and any number of other places with the same sociological construction.

But—to hark back. In the years surrounding World War I, the Fair Park area was the sports focal point of the city. The old Dallas Giants, owned by Joe Gardner and managed by Jim Maloney, played at Gaston Park there, and the heroes were guys like Harry Storch, a home run slugger who would stand in center field and throw the ball over the grandstand, and Heinie Magg and Les Tullos and a pesky bat boy named George Schepps, who later was to own and operate his own Dallas team. At the old Fair Park track, the great harness racer Dan Patch outpaced another fine horse, Minor Heir. This is where Barney Oldfield once pushed his race car through the dirt corners and where Harry Greb decisioned Johnny Celmars and where Frankie Fink started on his way to national featherweight prominence and Tom Beaupre boxed, and later, in the mid-thirties, where the thoroughbreds ran in that one brief exposure to horse racing in the state.

This also was to be site of the Cotton Bowl, a fantastic structure in 1930, seating an unbelievable 45,000.

The evolution of baseball saw Gardner move his team from Gaston Park to a new location on the west cliffs of the Trinity, Joe Gardner Park. It adjoined the first ice rink in the south, also owned by Gardner. The streetcar barns were nearby, and this was the favorite mode of transportation to the ball yard. That park burned, after a double-header against Wichita Falls in 1924. It was rebuilt as Steer Stadium and the team went through a succession of owners, Ham Patterson and Jesse Hassell, then Ike Sablosky, J. Walter Morris and George and Julius Schepps, then Tavener Lupton, then Fred McJunkin and Sol Dreyfuss. In 1938 George Schepps got control of the club, paying $150,000 for 84 per cent, and taking in some minor partners like brother Julius, Dan Rodgers, James K. Wilson, Pat Greenwood, Bob O'Donnell. Ten years later, a Texarkana oilman named Dick Burnett blew into town with a flask and a valise full of large coarse bank notes and shelled out a whopping $555,000 for the then-Rebels, highest sale for a minor league operation in baseball history.

The Cotton Bowl.

OPPOSITE:
Southern Methodist Mustangs.

Burnett, a rambunctious sort, is remembered for a couple of events. First, he moved his 1950 opening-day game to the Cotton Bowl because of its seating capacity, gathered famous baseball names from all over the country, and pulled 53,578 through the gates, largest minor league baseball crowd ever. Also, Burnett was the first to break the color line in the Texas League, signing a black pitcher, Dave Hoskins, in 1952.

Burnett died in 1957, when the bloom was beginning to fade from minor league baseball the nation over, and J. J. W. Bateson, a wealthy contractor, was the next owner. He and Fort Worth's Amon Carter, Jr., made a mighty effort to secure a major league franchise for North Texas, but were denied. (This was the first of two major league attempts before the third try became the charm. Ray Johnson was the next owner and he tried a hybrid Dallas–Fort Worth operation that flopped miserably. Lamar Hunt of Dallas and Tommy Murcer of Fort Worth then bought the team and moved it to a tidy little new stadium in Arlington, site of the current Texas Ranger major league team which came in 1972.

The minor league days were purely fun, gigged by intense rivalry between the Dallas Steers or Rebels or Eagles and the Fort Worth Cats. And there were always the familiar heroes year after year, Snipe Conley, Jerry Witte, the home run hitter, Red Murff, Buck Frierson, who hit the ball over the wall almost as often as he dropped fly balls in the outfield, Eddie Knoblauch, any number of popular old names.

Bob Short, the Washington Senator owner who moved his franchise here in 1972, two years later sold 90 per cent of the team to a local Dallas–Fort Worth combine of Brad Corbett, Ray Nasher, Charles Sharp, Bill Seay, Pollard Simon, Amon Carter, and a few others. It was fortunate timing for the locals, for this was the season when the Rangers gained prominence both in the standings and in the cash register. The club also went through a confusing procession of managers in that short span of three years—Ted Williams, Whitey Herzog, Billy Martin, and Frank Lucchesi.

The football history has been a bit checkered. Of course, the city has always been a high school hotbed, as most Texas towns, producing such glamour names as Father Lumpkin, Davey O'Brien, I. B. Hale, Doak Walker, Bobby Layne. In fact, only one city (Chicago) has produced more consensus All-America choices than Dallas' eight—Walker, Layne, O'Brien, J. D. Roberts, Dan and Hank Foldberg, Bud Sprague, and J. C. Wetsel.

The year of 1935 will live, like *Apollo 11*, forever in memories of those we now classify as old-timers. (At one time, of course, they were whippersnappers with soft, pliable memories.)

This was the SMU team of Bobby Wilson and Harry Shuford and Bob Finley, of Maurice Orr and Truman Spain. This was the season of the great confrontation with Sammy Baugh and his Texas Christian team. Both outfits were unbeaten, untied, and a Rose Bowl invitation awaited the winner. You may not remember yesterday's Roger Staubach pass to Golden Richards that beat the Redskins, but everybody remembers vividly Finley's long spiral to Bobby Wilson that won the massive struggle, 20–14, and made SMU the only Southwest team ever to play in a Rose Bowl. The Mustangs lost to Stanford in that game, but they had already been voted the Knute Rockne trophy, symbolic of the national collegiate championship in those days.

Next came the vibrant Doak Walker era, the three seasons of 1947–48–49 when the miraculous little halfback pulled all his patented clutch plays, runs, passes, kicks. He was not "the man who built the Cotton Bowl," as Yankee Stadium is so credited to Babe Ruth, but Doak is the man who enlarged it from that original 45,500 capacity to 67,431 his junior season, then 75,504 his senior year. He, of course, is the only three-time All-America the Southwest Conference ever produced, the Heisman Trophy winner who went on to professional stardom with the Detroit Lions, where he joined his old Highland Park teammate, Bobby Layne, who had become sidetracked at the University of Texas.

Tangled among those chronological events came the development of the annual Cotton Bowl game. This was an idea of Curtis Sanford, a local businessman and promoter. Sanford staged four of the games, starting in 1937, as a private enterprise before selling the idea for about $10,000 to a group of Dallas businessmen (Fred Florence, R. L. Thornton, Freeman Burford, Jake Hamon, and others), and these citizens then turned the game over to the Southwest Conference. It remains the only conference-operated bowl game in the country and has always featured the conference champion as the host team. The growth of the game in national prestige is perhaps best measured by its popularity on television, from $31,740 for radio-television rights in 1951 to a fee of $815,500 for the same rights in 1975.

The professional football operation in Dallas got off to a rocky start in 1952 when Giles and Connell Miller and associates brought the original Dallas Texans to town (they had been the New York Yankees). The project was a sad economic failure, and the National Football League office moved the franchise out of Dallas before the season ended. Those Dallas Texans, which included Buddy Young and Art Donovan, later became the world-champion Baltimore Colts.

When pro football returned, in 1960, it came in bunches. Lamar Hunt, of the H. L. Hunt oil millions, was a third-string end at SMU during the Doak Walker days, and he had a quiet but fierce interest in sports. Actually, not many of the city hierarchy knew much about Lamar nor—at that time—about his father, for they were a private family who shunned the glare.

Lamar had tried to obtain an NFL franchise but was told there was none available, so he became determined to organize his own professional football league. That he did, the American Football League, with offices in Dallas and Hunt's own Dallas Texans entrenched in the Cotton Bowl.

Then, in an unadmitted effort to squash the naïve new league, the old National Football League also established a new franchise in Dallas, selling it to another scion of a Dallas oil fortune, Clint Murchison, Jr. Oddly enough, these two wealthy young men had never met.

For three years, the two factions battled bitterly. The city was divided; banks,

Dallas Cowboys bossman, Coach Tom Landry.

businessmen, merchants, seemed caught in the switch. The country club set seemed to prefer the Cowboys; the blue-collar guy was in sympathy with the Texans. But neither team paid its way. Many otherwise interested sports customers, wearying of the bickering, simply stayed at home. A paid crowd of twenty thousand was exceptional, although neither team would admit actual paid attendance figures, to avoid embarrassment.

It became obvious that both teams couldn't survive, without putting a severe drain on the Murchison and Hunt coffers.

John Breen, then general manager of the Houston Oilers, surveyed the depressing Dallas situation and said, "They ought to flip a coin and the winner gets to leave town."

After the Texans won the AFL championship in 1962, Hunt did indeed move his franchise to Kansas City, carting away such local favorites as E. J. Holub, Abner Haynes, Jerry Mays, Johnny Robinson, et al. There was gossip at the time that Murchison paid Hunt a settlement to leave town, a report denied by both parties. Then there was another rumor that Hunt was given an option to buy into Cowboy ownership should he dispose of his Kansas City team. This, too, was denied.

Anyway, the Cowboys then gradually began to prosper, slowly building a contending team under Tex Schramm and Tom Landry, through a vast, modern, expensive scouting system. From a laughingstock to an NFL championship game against the old established Green Bay Packers in 1966 was quite a vault. And much to the national surprise, the Cowboys dang near won the thing. And they pulled a repeat act the next year, in the memorable Ice Bowl game on the Wisconsin tundra.

While the Cowboys were gaining muscle, they became the national darlings, everybody's favorite team, bludgeoned by fate and fortune, but still bouncing back bravely. It was at this particular time that sociologists could point to a heavy social contribution by sports. The rise of the Cowboys and the national sympathy and attention they attracted did much to blot a national stigma that had plagued the city since the Kennedy assassination in 1963.

This Cowboy reputation, however, lasted only a couple years, until the team began losing play-off games to Cleveland, then finally making it to the 1972 Super Bowl where they lost a comedy of errors to the Baltimore Colts. During that span, the Cowboys became known as "the team that couldn't win the big one," a defacing brand that was finally erased when Bob Lilly, Roger Staubach, Lee Roy Jordan, and friends won the 1973 Super Bowl over Miami.

The Cowboy path has not been cushiony, despite the Murchison millions and the experienced direction of Schramm and the "straight arrow" image of the coach, Tom Landry. There have been sordid incidents involving several players, public blasts at management by other players. And then there was the Big Stadium Hassle between Murchison and some of the more "influential" city dads. Basically, the savage split was between Murchison and State Fair administrators and its president, Bob Cullum, and the mayor at the time, Erik Jonsson. Murchison became disgusted at the aging Cotton Bowl and its location at Fair Park. He wanted the city to build

Byron Nelson Golf Classic. Lee Trevino at home on the links.

a new downtown stadium; he even plotted the location on the southwest sector of the business sector, conducted surveys, drew plans. Cullum pushed for a State Fair location, should a new stadium be built. Jonsson backed the State Fair premise. There was great bitterness on both sides, and, at times, the wrangle appeared of the kindergarten recess category.

Finally, Murchison despaired of fighting City Hall, went to the nearby city of Irving, and sold the new stadium idea there. Thus, Texas Stadium was built, a true showplace for football. But even then, controversy clung to the Cowboys like cockleburs. To help finance the stadium, Murchison ruled that any season ticket purchaser must first buy a $1,000 stadium bond if he wanted to sit between the thirty-yard lines or a $250 bond for any other stadium location. This plan infuriated some Cowboy faithful, and consequently, the Cowboys sell fewer season tickets (30,000–33,000) than any team in the league.

Too, the stadium top is ringed with private boxes that sell for $50,000 for the bare sixteen-by-sixteen space and that have been decorated lavishly by the purchasers. There the wealthy patrons sit, like Roman royalty, with their air conditioning, their closed-circuit television, their bartenders, adding to the country club atmosphere of the place. Some critics complain, with justification, that the warmth and enthusiasm generated at the old Cotton Bowl is missing at the cold and clinical Texas Stadium.

This widely recognized chilliness abruptly vanished in 1975, however, when a rather weird Cowboy team, a mixture of old-timers and wild and woolly rookies, somehow won the National Conference and made the team's third trip to the Super Bowl. This was a storybook season and was greeted in rambunctious fashion by a suddenly aroused populace, despite Dallas' narrow 21–17 loss to Pittsburgh in Super Bowl X.

The growth of Dallas golf has been another impressive yardstick of sports economics. The city now has seventeen country clubs, one of which (Preston Trail) has seen memberships sell for as high as $22,000. Another half-dozen country clubs are in suburban townships. Ten municipal courses are hereabouts. And the city's major golf event, the Byron Nelson Classic, has reached national stature, the eventual product of a tournament started by electronic whiz Jim Ling, back in 1956. The event had fairly rough sledding for several years when it was held at Oak Cliff Country Club, mainly because of sweltering late-summer dates forced on the tournament by the Professional Golf Association's scheduling committee. The tournament shifted gears, however, when the live-wire Salesmanship Club took over the sponsorship, moved play to Preston Trail Golf Club north of town, and named it after the city's favorite golf personality, Byron Nelson.

The tournament is always on national television, and its 1970 climax, with Jack Nicklaus and Arnold Palmer tying and going into a sudden-death play-off (which Nicklaus won), will remain a classic.

At one time in the 1960s, Dallas also was home base for many touring pros— Tony Lema, Gay Brewer, Don January, Billy Maxwell, Jack Cupit, John Schlee, Ray Floyd, Doug Sanders, Bob Charles, Bruce Crampton, Don Massingale, Billy Martindale—because of the year-round weather, the abundance of good golf courses, and the airline connections.

Other sports ventures have not been so fortunate. Failure of the original Dallas Texans has been mentioned. Pro basketball, seemingly upholstered by some of the thickest young wallets in the city, was a bummer. After six losing seasons, both on the court and at the cash register, the Dallas Chaparrals of the American Basketball Association gave up the fight and moved to San Antonio, where there was no pro sports competition. Eventually the team was sold to a group of San Antonio investors.

Professional boxing has struggled also. There was an ancient day when it was a feature of Fair Park, when Jack Dillion fought Paul Romans and Pete Latzo boxed Clyde Hull, and a local featherweight, Frankie Fink, started on his career that was to take him to Madison Square Garden. Curtis Cokes, a native, won the world welterweight championship by beating Manuel Gonzalez in New Orleans in 1966. Cokes held the title three years, defending it three times in his home town's Memorial Auditorium, but the matches were not overwhelming box-office successes.

The city has spawned many excellent amateur fighters, such as Pat Riley, who won the national Golden Gloves flyweight title in the late forties, and James Martinez, who twice won national Golden Gloves championships a quarter century later. And Johnny O'Glee, Carl Hilger, Jackie Blair, who fought Willie Pep a couple times, Jackie Woodruff, Dickie Cole, Burt and Gene Gilliam, Chuck Simmons.

Lamar Hunt, who founded the American Football League and who was instrumental (along with the Cowboys' Tex Schramm) in effecting the merger with the NFL, has become internationally recognized as a sports investor, and a couple of his projects have left imprints on his home city. Other than the Dallas Texans, now the Kansas City Chiefs, Hunt controls the World Championship of Tennis tour and he stages the WCT singles championship, involving the eight highest finishers of the

Chris Evert at Maureen Connally Brinker Tourney.

WCT tour, each spring at Moody Coliseum on the SMU campus. This event has become internationally recognized, attracts press coverage from all over Europe, and is simply called "Dallas" by the players, just as the British Open championship matches are called "Wimbledon" and the U. S. Open is referred to as "Forest Hills." The 1971 finals match, in which Ken Rosewall finally beat Rod Laver, has been classified as one of tennis' all-time great moments.

Hunt was also involved in an ill-fated national bowling league and built a bowling establishment with a separate amphitheater for league matches. Moreover, Hunt was the driving force behind introduction of professional soccer to this country. His Dallas Tornado has been considerably less than a howling success in attendance, but the club's youth program has some forty thousand children playing soccer in the city and the sport has become part of the public schools' athletic curriculum.

The future?

The Texas Rangers of the American Baseball League at their home field in Arlington Stadium.

Professional basketball and big league hockey are most probably on the horizon; they could be considered certainties if an indoor arena of about eighteen thousand capacity is built. However, the arena may have to be financed privately, for city dads and city voters don't seem at all enthused about a bond issue to fund same. And private financing isn't exactly the easiest game in town.

The sports personality of Dallas has changed drastically in the last half century. No longer is the city a provincial, united fandom. Some 27 per cent of the population is from out of state, so therefore the sports interest is much more varied. Neither is SMU the dominant force it once was. There are probably more University of Texas exes and supporters within city boundaries than SMU sympathizers.

As Dallas enters the downhill side of the seventies, the baseball Rangers seem to be making inroads on the established income of the Cowboys, possibly because of the football players strike and the continual hassle between union and management, plus the increasing ticket prices (two hikes totaling three dollars in a two-year span). Pro football may find the going a bit steeper in the next decade unless, of course, pay television comes into universal acceptance. That could be the answer to sports financing in Dallas, as in every other city in the country. Even the frustrated ones.

DALLAS
THROUGH THE SEASONS

175

Dr. Bill J. Priest, the chancellor of the Dallas County Community College District since 1965, came to Dallas from Sacramento, California, where he had established a reputation that won him national recognition as president of the American Association of Junior Colleges in 1966.

Born in French Camp, California, in 1917, he received his B.A., M.A., and doctoral degrees at the University of California, Berkeley. In 1941 he married Marietta Shaw. During World War II he served with the U. S. Navy as an intelligence officer and holds the rank of captain (ret.) in the U. S. Naval Reserve.

Dr. Priest's active participation in state and national education organizations and his civic interests and positions are commensurate with his leadership.

Education

by DR. BILL J. PRIEST

Specific details about the beginnings of education in the city of Dallas are hard to come by. As was true in many frontier towns of the 1840s and 1850s, education, like Topsy, "just grew," because parents recognized that their progeny needed some type of training and set about arranging it. Isacc Webb's Home School, which opened in 1845, was apparently the initial effort to provide education in Dallas. The following year, 1846, a public school was opened at Cedar Springs and Oak Lawn.

Although Texas laws, as early as 1841, provided subventions for the public schools, the allocation was so small that the impact was negligible. By 1859, however, according to newspaper accounts of that period, some seven schools were in operation in the village of Dallas. Costs were largely defrayed by a modest tuition, with the rate corresponding to the type of education received.

It was 1882 before the citizens saw fit to levy a school tax against the local property to support education. Interestingly enough, this preceded by two years the establishment of a local Board of Education to govern the institutions funded from such tax. Financial records for the school year 1883–84 reveal that the Dallas schools received $598.40 from the County Fund and a $7,920.00 allocation from the state, making a grand total of $8,510.40 available for school operation.

From 1884 to 1921 Dallas provided public education through the high school grades in much the same way as other communities in the region. However, during the 1920s the city apparently forged ahead of some of the more prosaic systems and introduced a number of innovations that identified it as a leader in public education in the area, if not the nation. These innovations included the use of portable buildings, the introduction of special education programs, and the development of the team teaching method of instruction.

Significant leadership was provided by Dallasites in developing a legal framework in which Texas school districts could break away from municipal control and function as independent political subdivisions of the state. Efforts to accomplish this separation were begun in 1923, but the matter was not concluded until 1947 when independent school districts became a legal reality. Concurrent with this development of public education was the creation of a number of private schools, some of which gained considerable prestige among the citizens who could afford to send their children to tuition-assessing institutions. Two primary factors contributed to this high standing. First was the elite status assigned to sending one's children to private schools. Secondly it was popularly held that the quality of private education was superior to the public offerings. Features of the private schools that contributed to this viewpoint included restrictive admission standards, low student-teacher ratios, and highly trained instructors who placed considerable emphasis on individualizing the learning experience.

The Terrill Preparatory School, founded in 1906 by Mentor B. Terrill, was such an institution. Its claim to fame was that it was patterned with considerable fidelity after the type of school one might find in the East, where educators of the day were alleged to be well informed about the operation of prep schools. Hockaday for girls and St. Mark's (formerly Texas Country Day School) for boys were other such ventures. These two institutions have continued to thrive and still enjoy a fine reputation in the Dallas educational community. No doubt the Ivy League syndrome that is apparent in Dallas had its seeds in these institutions.

Certainly stability of leadership is one of the noticeable elements in a review of public education in the city of Dallas, especially in recent years. A total of eight superintendents served the Dallas Independent School District between 1884 and 1924. At this juncture the turnover slowed down markedly, and from 1924 to 1968 there were only three superintendents at the helm. This stability was remarkable in light of the increased pressures of the times. W. T. White served from 1945 to 1968, with all the concomitant problems in education one might expect. His successor, Nolan Estes, has held the post since 1968, dealing with a complex of problems brought about by shifting populations and increasing judicial involvement.

Which Dallas school a child attended was determined by the location of his family home. The emphasis placed upon the neighborhood school concept created a condition that precipitated separation of not only ethnic groups but social and economic classes as well. Generally speaking, attendance at a particular school reflected the economic standing of the family. This was less apparent as people became more mobile and population centers of the city shifted.

For most children, school attendance began at the first-grade level, for it was not until 1970–71 that the state of Texas recognized kindergarten as a legitimate school class and appropriated funds for its support.

Dallas' rapid growth from country town to a major metropolitan area had its effect on the schools. It was typical in predominately rural Texas for each commu-

nity to have one major school to which the town expressed its loyalty. As Dallas grew so did its school system and with it the development of school rivalries. The growth of the public school system is dramatized by the following statistics, which span ninety years:

	1885	1965	1975
Number of schools	6	170	184*
Enrollment	1,457	154,707	144,384
Cost per pupil	——	(est.) $360	$991
Budget	$13,144.83	$76,359,310	$202,869,362

In 1975 the total physical plant consisted of 205 buildings valued at $275 million. Some outstanding features of the Dallas public schools included:

*Source: DISD Publication, 1975–76, "Credit Your Schools With Progress."

- Bilingual education programs in twenty-nine elementary schools
- Affirmative Action program
- A revamped curriculum which emphasizes relevance to adult life
- A comprehensive swimming program which operates year round at seven district-owned pools
- Skyline Center, a nationally famous high school completed in 1971, costing over $21,000,000 and providing career and adult education programs
- Eighty-two separate career education programs
- District-wide average teacher/student ratio of 1:27
- Drug abuse education program
- Physical education courses encouraging lifelong participation in exercise and recreation
- Multi-cultural social studies courses
- A communication headquarters called Action Center, which provides answers to citizens on questions concerning the district

Until very recent years, efforts in Dallas to provide training beyond the high school level were comparatively modest when one considers the size of the population and the educational needs of the period. The first recorded effort in the field of higher education was the founding of the Dallas Male and Female College in 1863. In 1869 a second institution, the Dallas Female College, was opened. Despite its name this was a coeducational institution. During the 1870s, '80s, and '90s a number of private and sectarian post-high school institutions came into being, but failed to survive.

The Dallas pattern was typical of many in the region during this particular period of American history, but, contrary to the experiences of some cities, where major universities subsequently evolved from such modest beginnings, none of the early Dallas colleges grew into a distinguished national institution of higher learning. It is also true that while higher education was plodding along in a comparatively undistinguished manner, Dallas was moving ahead as a center of finance and industry. The record gives credibility to the allegation that Dallasites have focused rather intently on making money at the expense of progress on the educational and cultural fronts.

An event that was to have significant impact on Dallas higher education occurred in 1908 when the Methodists lost control of Vanderbilt University in Nashville, Tennessee. The church leadership immediately cast about to find a location for a new college to fill the role formerly played by Vanderbilt. Rather keen competition developed among cities vying for this new institution. Among the front-runners in consideration were Dallas and Fort Worth. Various overtures were made toward the Methodist hierarchy, and the decision zigged and zagged for several years. Finally the die was cast when W. W. Caruth, of Dallas, gave sixty-eight acres to the

196

Lillian Bradshaw, director, Dallas Public Libraries.

Dr. Louise Cowan, guiding spirit of the University of Dallas.

Ela Hockaday, founder of the famed Hockaday School for Girls in Dallas in 1913, was born in Ladonia, Texas, in 1875. After early schooling in Bonham, Texas, she graduated from the Denton Normal School (now North Texas State University) and did graduate work at Columbia University and the University of Chicago.

Like her pioneer schoolteacher father, she was dedicated to education in the broadest sense of the word and began her own teaching career in Sherman, Texas, but was soon invited to head the Department of Biology at Oklahoma State Normal School. Later she joined the faculty of Oklahoma College for Women.

At the suggestion of M. B. Terrill, of the Terrill School for Boys in Dallas, Miss Hockaday was urged by certain Dallas residents to come and open a preparatory school of highest quality education for girls. This she did, and its success has involved steady expansion in size and operation ever since. She retired in 1946 and died in 1956. COURTESY OF HOCKADAY SCHOOL.

Mrs. Henry Exall, Sr., a Vassar girl, came to Dallas from McKinney, Texas, in 1883. Not content as socialite wife of the president of the first million-dollar bank in Texas, she became the first president of the Dallas Shakespeare Club in 1886 and held that office for over fifty years. She also organized the Dallas Woman's Club in 1922 and later the Dallas Federation of Women's Clubs. It was her contact with Andrew Carnegie that established the Dallas Public Library, and she led her friends to contribute enough to commission the equestrian sculpture of General Robert E. Lee for Lee Park. Her own portrait by Douglas Chandor was a presentation of the Dallas Shakespeare Club to honor her pioneer leadership of women in Dallas. COURTESY OF THE DALLAS WOMAN'S CLUB.

SECOND ROW:

World-famous as one of America's libraries most noted for its ability to present the evolution of the book from the origin of printing onward, Bridwell Library at Perkins School of Theology, Southern Methodist Univeristy, is a treasury of rare collections.

Seen here is Dr. Decherd Turner, its director, with the library's copy of the first complete Bible printed in English, the 1535 Miles Coverdale translation.

Eugene McDermott, GITTINGS.

Latest among the great libraries of special collections in the Dallas area is the Eugene McDermott Library on the campus of the University of Texas at Dallas.

Among its 500,000 volumes are the Berkner Collection in science, the Lundell Collection in earth and life sciences, and the Green Collection on Central and South America cultures. Mr. James Dodson is director.

The library is the most appropriate living memorial among many of the vast philanthropies of Eugene McDermott, whose whole life was a personal commitment to the basic harmony of science, industry, the arts, and scholarship.

THIRD ROW:

The DeGolyer Foundation Library, located on the Southern Methodist University campus and directed by Everett L. DeGolyer, Jr., pictured here, offers the public some 90,000 books, prints, and related materials of highly specialized collections on the Trans-Mississippi West, Mexico, and Canada in history, economics, business and industry, transportation, and geology. Some 30,000 of the volumes on geology are in the Science Information Library.

This distinctive collection was begun in 1912 by Everett L. DeGolyer, Sr. (1886–1956), whose bequest together with his wife's gift established the Foundation Library in 1957. Everett DeGolyer, Jr., began his collection in 1935 and actively continues to add to it. Dr. Jim Phillips is master cataloguer.

Born in Fannin County in 1894, Hastings Harrison, a layman who accomplished more for brotherhood than if he had been in the clergy, rose from farm boy through Trinity University to schoolteacher, executive director of several YMCAs, and then regional and national leadership in the National Conference of Christians and Jews. "I have always abhorred bigotry and intolerance and the stereotyping of human beings," he has repeatedly stated. In 1975 he retired after sixteen years as consultant to the president of Southern Methodist University. In the Owen Art Center on campus the Instrumental and Choral Halls have been named for him to honor his works.

Methodist group and added to this outright gift a one-half interest in an additional 722 acres. This inducement turned the trick, and Dallas was selected. Additional funding was obtained from a number of donors, and in 1911 Dr. R. S. Hyer was employed to establish what was to become Southern Methodist University. Construction started on the original building, Dallas Hall, in 1912. The doors were opened in 1915 to the first student body of 706 enrollees, who attended classes in the two buildings completed at that time.

In the fall of 1975, 9,643 students matriculated at SMU. Its physical plant had grown to eighty buildings and 155 acres with a valuation of $82 million. Six hundred sixty-two faculty members served in the university's eight schools: University College, Meadows School of the Arts, Business Administration, Humanities and Sciences, Law, Institute of Technology, Continuing Education, and the Perkins School of Theology. Studies leading to 237 bachelor's, master's, and doctoral degrees were offered in 110 fields of study.

Students could choose from a variety of educational majors, nontraditional combinations, and interdisciplinary programs. In addition, SMU enrolled eighty-five to ninety students in the three-year degree program, which reduced the required time of the typical bachelor's degree by one year.

SMU was not established to provide education beyond high school for large numbers of residents of the greater Dallas area. Rather, it was a regional sectarian institution, characterized by substantial tuition fees and a selective admissions policy. Therefore, there continued to exist in Dallas a sizable vacuum in higher education. This vacuum continued for many years but was countered by interesting

Edward H. Cary, a successful young salesman, came to Dallas from Alabama to join his brother, A. P. Cary, in the dental supplies business, but he had so much trouble with his eyes that he decided to become an ophthalmologist. In 1895 the twenty-three-year-old salesman enrolled at Bellevue Hospital Medical College, interning there and also at the New York Eye and Ear Infirmary. In 1901 Dr. Cary was in practice in Dallas, and a year later he was dean of the University of Dallas Medical Department, the first local medical school, founded by Dr. Charles Rosser. Dr. Cary led this school into Baylor University at Waco in 1903, the year of planning the Texas Baptist Memorial Sanatorium in Dallas. This later became Baylor University Hospital, with Dr. Cary as dean. After many regional honors he became president of the American Medical Association in 1932. He was responsible for the erection of the Medical Arts Building in downtown Dallas and in 1939 was among the incorporators of the Southwestern Medical Foundation. His wife was Georgia Fonda Schneider, daughter of a pioneer Texas family. Dr. Cary died in 1953.

forces, chief of which was a heavy reliance on perimeter schools. Among these were the public junior college at Arlington, which subsequently became a branch of the University of Texas and expanded into a complete university; East Texas State University, which, though some sixty miles away, attracted large numbers of Dallas residents; and North Texas State University and College of Industrial Arts (later Texas Woman's University), only thirty miles away in Denton, where hordes of Dallasites have traveled for comparatively low-cost higher education. Earlier Dallas students went sixty miles north to Kidd-Key College in Sherman until its closing in 1935.

Although there are many examples of fine educational endeavors in the state of Texas, Texas has not historically been a national leader in higher education. For many years only Rice University could be characterized as a nationally prestigious university. Since the end of World War II a change has been taking place, and if one were to pick the most prestigious institution in the state of Texas today, it would have to be the University of Texas in Austin.

A number of additional projects in the area of higher education are certainly worthy of mention in any over-all treatment of education in the Dallas area. A good example is the Southwestern Medical School, which ranks high among America's leading medical training centers. This is a comparatively new institution which has made meteoric progress since it was established in 1943. After the Medical School had operated six years with funding from the original foundation that created it, the University of Texas assumed control, and it became an appendage of this state-wide public higher education system. However, substantial financial support for both facilities and operational costs continues to come from the private sector.

Bishop College, which had operated in Marshall, Texas, since its founding in 1881 by black Baptist groups, was induced to move to Dallas early in the 1960s. Bishop College is a four-year liberal arts institution which derives its income from church support, tuition, and private donors. With Carr Collins, local philanthropist, acting as the main sponsor, funds were raised that permitted the development of five new buildings. Federal funding also was made available for this project. Since moving to Dallas, Bishop College has grown from a modest 640 students in its opening year to approximately 1,700 students in 1975. Its student body is predominately black; its faculty is approximately 50 per cent black.

Another church-connected college that came into Dallas in the mid-1960s is Dallas Baptist College. This institution was established in Decatur in 1897 as a private junior college. After operating initially in Dallas as a private two-year liberal arts college, it added two additional years in 1968 and 1969 and moved to a fine new campus in the western part of the city. DBC has suffered rather severe financial troubles, but there is hope in its struggle for survival now.

The University of Dallas, a Catholic four-year liberal arts school, was founded in 1955. Although it is located in Irving rather than in the city of Dallas, it must be regarded as a part of the educational community of the greater Dallas area. It is an institution of modest size, 1,200–1,500 students, and has shown no visible trend

LEFT: Richland College. BELOW: Eastfield College.
OPPOSITE, ABOVE: Hockaday School. BELOW: St. Mark's School.

The University of Dallas.   The University of Texas at Dallas.

toward rapid expansion. University of Dallas funding has been obtained from several sources, chief of which are major donors for the physical facility costs plus contributors to the endowment from which operational expenses may be derived. Tuition, however, continues to be one of its main sources of operating funds.

A new institution in Dallas is the University of Texas at Dallas. This institution had its beginning in an unusual educational experiment conducted by three imaginative industrial leaders: Cecil Green, Erik Jonsson, and Eugene McDermott. On the premise that industry could not prosper without an adequate supply of high-level scientific brain power, and observing that the Dallas area was dependent upon outside recruitment for such commodity, the decision was made to create a local production line for scientific talent. The instrument to achieve this was a privately funded research and training center known as the Graduate Research Center of the Southwest, later renamed the Southwest Center for Advanced Studies. Although the experiment was successful in many respects, it became apparent that the funding needed to support an enterprise of this magnitude exceeded that which could be made available from private sources. This fact, plus a belief that a population center such as Dallas was entitled to a branch of the state university, ultimately produced the University of Texas at Dallas, an upper-level university that begins at the junior year and provides graduate programs through the doctoral level. UTD enrolled its first undergraduate students in the fall of 1975.

During the early 1960s, attention was directed toward the establishment of a community college district or districts in the greater Dallas area. Serious steps to establish such a system were taken by the Richardson Independent School District and the Dallas Independent School District, but were not carried to conclusion, for various reasons. A number of studies were conducted by such groups as the Chamber of Commerce and the League of Women Voters and by independent citizens. The upshot was a concerted effort to develop a county-wide community/junior college system.

This was accomplished in May 1965, when the voters of the county created a new district and provided for other legal and financial details. This district, now known

as the Dallas County Community College District, began serving the citizenry in 1966 when El Centro College was opened in a remodeled downtown building. Response was immediate and overwhelming, and three additional campuses were created in the suburban area of Dallas.

Two of these, Mountain View College and Eastfield College, opened in 1970; a third, Richland College, was opened in 1972. In line with a timetable established as a result of an earlier comprehensive study, a major bond campaign was staged in 1972. Funding was authorized for the three additional campuses that would round out the seven-campus complex provided for in the District Master Plan. In consonance with this plan, Cedar Valley and North Lake College are scheduled to open in 1977, followed by Brookhaven College in 1978.

During the 1974–75 school year, more than 60,000 students enrolled in the four operating colleges. Forecasts indicate that this number will exceed 100,000 by the middle or late 1980s. All seven of these institutions are scheduled to be comprehensive community colleges, their mission being identified in four areas: transfer education, occupational training, counseling and guidance, and community service/adult education.

Already these institutions are the single largest source of sophisticated manpower in the North Texas area. When the seven-campus complex is completed, no resident of Dallas County will be more than fifteen minutes from a college, and the goal of readily available, low-cost quality college education will be realized.

Despite the comparative stability of Dallas, there was, during the late 1960s and early 1970s, a running battle between conservatives and liberals for control of the Dallas Independent School District Board of Trustees. The generally conservative Committee for Good Schools, with a record of dominating DISD board elections for decades, was challenged by the liberal League for Educational Advancement in Dallas. Very active campaigns were organized by both groups, and control of the board shifted back and forth between CGS and LEAD. This ideological struggle continues, although it is now focusing more on issues than personalities.

So brief an account of Dallas education cannot hope to treat the problem of school desegregation in any substantial manner. However, it would be impossible to speak to the question of education in Dallas and ignore this crucial issue.

Dallas, like almost every other major American city, has primarily a segregated housing pattern. Like other southern cities, it also had a *de jure* system of school segregation prior to the Supreme Court decision in 1954. Efforts to change *de facto* segregation and the traditional inherited attitudes of citizens through alteration of the law have not been monumental successes. There is evidence that in Dallas, as in many other American cities, too much attention has been given to attacking the symptoms and too little to attacking the disease.

Certainly the busing issue comes squarely under this generalization. Its battleground has been the courts, and the adversaries appear to be the Dallas Independent School District and certain plaintiffs who allege that contemporary practices regarding segregation in this district do not conform to law. The courts, obviously confused by the complexity of the problem and the unanticipated consequences of earlier court decisions, seem to find their most effective response to be silence or delay. This produces anxiety and hostility within the public at large and tends to exaggerate the differences among the citizenry.

Although busing is only one of many broad issues involved in this complex matter, it seems to evoke more emotionalism than any other element. The white flight that tends to accompany integration and massive busing has implications extending far beyond the field of public education. The economic and sociological implications in themselves pose problems of great magnitude which will influence the very fiber of a community.

At this time the "jury is still out," and how the battle will end up is anyone's guess. Meanwhile, there is great instability, hostility, and confusion, none of which is designed to strengthen a city and its people.

Any account of education in Dallas that failed to recognize the individuals who provided leadership would be incomplete. Limitations of space, however, preclude more than identification of a few of the many fine citizens who have given of themselves or their resources to promote educational opportunity for Dallasites. There follows a list of institutions and prime movers whose names are inextricably interwoven with the creation and progress of such institutions:

BISHOP COLLEGE—Carr Collins, Fred Lange, M. B. Zale

DALLAS BAPTIST COLLEGE—Carr Collins

DALLAS COUNTY COMMUNITY COLLEGE DISTRICT—
R. L. Thornton, Jr., Margaret McDermott

DALLAS INDEPENDENT SCHOOL DISTRICT—W. T. White

SOUTHERN METHODIST UNIVERSITY—W. W. Caruth, Umphrey Lee,
Willis Tate

SOUTHWESTERN MEDICAL SCHOOL (UT)—Karl Hoblitzelle, Edward Cary

UNIVERSITY OF DALLAS—Edward Maher, Eugene Constantin, Erik
Jonsson, Eugene McDermott

UNIVERSITY OF TEXAS AT DALLAS—Erik Jonsson, Eugene McDermott,
Cecil Green

Whatever the future brings, public and private education at all levels does play
and will continue to play an important role in the community life of Dallas. This is
a city whose greatness has been influenced more by creative, imaginative, hard-
working people than by geographical or historical factors. The evolution of education to whatever position of eminence it enjoys here has been profoundly influenced
by the same kind of force—creative, imaginative, hard-working people.

Toni Beck has not one but two public profiles. Many people identify her with the Green-house, that famed spa on the Dallas–Fort Worth turnpike, where she is the director of exercise. But her regimen at the Greenhouse, as well as the exercise books she co-authored with Patsy Swank, are useful but not primary endeavors with Ms. Beck. Her consuming interest is modern dance, and in almost every city outside Dallas she is known for her skill in developing young dancers. She created the dance department at SMU which she now chairs. Her graduates go on to the great companies. Ms. Beck herself is in great demand abroad as a visiting choreographer. A former student of Martha Graham, Alwin Nikolais, Aubrey Hitchins, and Alexandra Danilova, Ms. Beck has performed in off-Broadway and Broadway musical comedies and plays, as well as for television. B.A. Oberlin College, M.A. Columbia University; Ford Foundation and Danforth grants in dance and choreography.

The Arts—Fine and Performing

by TONI BECK

I arrived in Dallas in 1954—an apprehensive "Easterner" who felt that all cultural activity centered around New York City. What I found was rather exciting. Activity was rampant—I remember attending the Dallas Symphony Orchestra concerts under the direction of Walter Hendl, being involved and energized by the Margo Jones theater-in-the-round, teaching at the Edith James Studio of Ballet, and performing in the Dallas State Fair Musicals' summer season under Charles Meeker. What more could a transplanted New Yorker want? There was much to be done and I felt that I could contribute in some small way to the vibrancy of the cultural life of Dallas.

My first task was to contact John Rosenfield, amusements editor of the Dallas *Morning News.* He guided me in terms of my work—modern dance—and began to plant seeds for me to be productive. It was exciting to be part of so much potential. I joined the Edith James Studio as a part-time teacher and began to build a small interest in contemporary dance. It was slow and plodding, but I did not mind.

Twenty-two years later I am still here, now chairman of the Dance Division at Southern Methodist University. I love Dallas—the freedom it offers one, the individuality and life-style that the city projects. But what has happened to the arts since my arrival and what will be their future? I came at a high point in the cultural life of the city and it has been downhill ever since. I am sure it will change as a new impetus is made in some direction. I have faith in this, but at present we are betwixt and between. I find myself going away from the community for stimulation. I find myself restless at the inactivity that is manifesting itself in all the arts—or perhaps, instead of inactivity, the repeat of well-known patterns of activity rather than challenging new outlets. How much easier it is for us to see a "tried and true" drama like Thornton Wilder's *Skin of Our Teeth* rather than a new untried work, or

to hear Beethoven's Ninth Symphony than a Stravinsky piece, or to see *Swan Lake* rather than a Balanchine work. We know what to expect from the classics, but do we want to expand our vision to include more areas of exploration? I think this is the problem of the arts in Dallas. And perhaps this is why there is a kind of stasis—a pause—at present.

I know that Dallas is a young city, and growth is never continuous but sporadic. As I survey our brief history I am looking for the key to our cultural growth. I return to the past to find keys to the future.

In tracing the history of the arts, I see a pattern emerging—that spurts of activity were made possible by strong-minded, determined artists encouraged by certain businessmen who believed in them and the good they were doing for Dallas. The artist was a dreamer, and the dream was made possible by some farsighted person or persons. Dallas' character changed about 1939 from a small intimate community into an emerging city. The early leaders felt it was their responsibility to give the people as much as possible—to make the people see the importance of the arts to the spirit of the city. There was universal pride in what was happening. Today, this kind of viable leadership is no longer present—pride in the city seems to be not as important as personal gain.

As we delve into the past I feel it important to mention a few of the ardent supporters and some of the "movers" in the arts. These were the people who contributed so much and propelled action.

BUSINESSMEN:

Eli Sanger—Civic Music Association

Karl Hoblitzelle—civic leader and philanthropist, president of Interstate Circuit, contributor to the Dallas Museum of Fine Arts

Waldo Stewart—Dallas Theater Center

Eugene and Margaret McDermott—Dallas Museum of Fine Arts, Margo Jones Theater

Mayor Robert L. Thornton—spirit of individuality and determination to make Dallas an important city

Algur Meadows—Dallas Museum of Fine Arts, Meadows Museum

Arthur Kramer, Sr., and Arthur Kramer, Jr.—Dallas Grand Opera Association

MOVERS:

Elmer Scott—director of the Civic Federation, supportive of all local functions in education and the arts using the federation's facilities for activities

Paul Van Katwijk—first professional conductor, Dallas Symphony Orchestra, 1929-42

Owen Fine Arts Center at SMU.

Lawrence Kelly—producer and manager of the Dallas Civic Opera, 1957–74

Margo Jones—manager and director of the Margo Jones Theater, 1947–55

Paul Baker—managing director of the Dallas Theater Center, from 1959

Jac Alder and Norma Young—Theatre Three, from 1961

Antal Dorati—conductor of the Dallas Symphony Orchestra, 1945–49

Walter Hendl—conductor of the Dallas Symphony Orchestra, 1949–58

Douglas MacAgy—director and curator of the Dallas Museum of Contemporary Arts, 1959–63

It was this combination of financial support plus the integrity and fanaticism of the dreamers that made the arts prosper and explode at certain intervals in Dallas' short history.

Along with the above there was a special person who acted as catalyst both for the community and for the dreamer. John Rosenfield became amusements editor of the Dallas *Morning News* in late 1925 and pushed the arts forward until his death in 1966. With Rosenfield's guidance and prodding, theater, music, dance, and fine art became important as Dallas passed from a provincial town to a metropolis. John pushed for quality and integrity. He believed that Dallas, as an evolving city, must have the arts—and the arts at their best—in order to survive.

THEATER

When we talk about theater and Dallas, the first thing that comes to mind is the dynamic and volatile Margo Jones who had a dream and made it a reality. In 1947 Margo Jones from Livingston, Texas, formed a professional theater dedicated to giving new plays a hearing. It took two years for it to happen, but with the guidance of John Rosenfield and the support of Eugene McDermott, who was president of the Margo Jones Board of Directors for ten years, a theater-in-the-round appeared at Fair Park in the Gulf Oil Playhouse. The success of the endeavor was largely due to her energy and enthusiasm, and when she died suddenly in 1955, the Margo Jones Theater foundered for two years—its energy gone—and died. Along with the idea of giving new scripts a chance to be seen, she presented a classic revival as well. The novelty of having a theater-in-the-round caught on. With the premiers of such plays as Tennessee Williams' *Summer and Smoke,* Joseph Hayes' *Leaf and Bough,* and Jerome Lawrence and Robert Lee's *Inherit the Wind,* the Margo Jones Theater received nationwide coverage and publicity. She ran her theater autocratically, but she still believed strongly in the creativity of theater artists. Thornton Wilder called her "a fighter, a builder, explorer, a mixer of truth and magic."

Theater was ever present in Dallas. In 1873 there was the Field Theater, which later changed to the Dallas Opera House in 1883. Audiences were entertained by touring performances of Sarah Bernhardt, Edwin Booth, Richard Mansfield, Clara Morris, and Lawrence Barrett; musical comedies and vaudeville were very popular. In 1901 the Opera House was destroyed by fire and a new structure was completed in 1904. For twenty years this theater was the leading host to theatrical troupes. By World War I the road show disappeared.

The first Dallas Little Theatre formation began in 1920 and was organized in the First Unitarian Church. From 1920–43 the Little Theatre thrived. As John William Rogers, himself a Dallas dramatist of repute, states in *The Lusty Texans of Dallas,* "The Little Theatre is the only community participation in a serious art form which sprang up, flourished and then passed so completely out of existence as to form a closed chapter in the cultural expression of the town and already to belong to history."

In 1925 Oliver Hindsell came to the front as director of the Dallas Little Theatre. Mr. Hindsell was adept at taking recent plays from the Broadway stage and reproducing them here with comparable excellence. The Dallas Little Theatre attracted national attention by winning the Belasco Cup in the National Little Theatre tournament three times. The theater moved in 1928 to a new building on Maple Avenue, and Hindsell left in 1931 for Hollywood. Charles Meredith became director in 1931 but left for Hollywood in 1938. During World War II the theater closed, and it wasn't until 1947 that Dallas saw it reopen under David Russell's direction. But the times were "out of joint" and the Little Theatre didn't survive.

The Dallas Theater Center, under the managing directorship of Paul Baker, has been in existence since 1959, housed in a theater designed by Frank Lloyd Wright. It is not a professional program. Mr. Baker envisaged the theater as a laboratory where the best trained talent from every corner of the world could serve dramatic internship. He regards the center not as a school in the academic sense but rather as a studio in the European sense with an apprentice artist/performing artist relationship. The repertory system is the heart of the Theater Center's program. It mixes contemporary plays with the classics, and a resident company has been established. This company is paid for performing and teaching as well. The casts are made up of the basic salaried professionals along with students.

It is rare when a native talent is recognized and encouraged in its own community. And indeed, it taxes credulity to say that the artist was a playwright who found not only a stage in Dallas, Texas, but an appreciative audience as well. Such was the fortune of Preston Jones.

For years, Jones had labored in Paul Baker's vineyard as an actor and director. All of a sudden, it seemed, he bloomed as a playwright, producing a trilogy of plays which the Theater Center mounted during the 1974–75 season. The word spread, and critics from New York and London came to praise what Jones had wrought. What he brought to the theater was West Texas. A sense of a place passed by and of a people as starved as their towns for attention. The Texas Trilogy included *Lu Ann Hampton Laverty Oberlander, The Last Meeting of the Knights of the White Magnolia,* and *Oldest Living Graduate.* The trilogy went on to the Kennedy Center in Washington, where it was produced to superb reviews in the spring of 1976.

Theatre Three, another community theater program, was founded in 1961. The original leaders were Jac Alder, Norma Young, Ester Ragland, and Bob Dracup. Starting in a makeshift theater and finally having its own house in the quadrangle on Routh Street, it presents current dramas, comedies, and musicals to the Dallas public. Mobil Oil has been its largest supporter. By 1974 the Dallas community had accepted Theatre Three and has contributed to its support along with grants from the National Endowment for the Arts. At present, Jac Alder is managing director and Norma Young is artistic director. The company is considered professional, although the entire cast does not have to be members of Actor's Equity.

In the late 1960s and early '70s, a plethora of dinner theaters arose, offering adequate food and popular entertainment at reasonable prices. The Windmill, Crystal Palace, Granny's, Gran' Crystal Palace, and others offer light comedies and musicals in compact versions with professional performers. It is pleasant entertainment, if not art.

The Dallas Summer Musicals have added summer excitement to Dallas for the past thirty-five years. The first professional season was in 1941 outside in the Bandshell. The original name was the Starlight Operettas, which was changed to the Dallas State Fair Musicals, and finally to the Dallas Summer Musicals. Charles Meeker was managing director from 1941 to 1959. He instigated the growth of musical theater on a highly professional level and brought the top professionals from the Broadway musical stage to appear. Meeker was supported enthusiastically by Robert L. Thornton, who was president of the State Fair of Texas and chairman of the Fair Board at that time. In 1960 Tom Hughes assumed the managing directorship and has continued to present a wide range of musicals for Dallas audiences.

THE ART OF THE CINEMA

Today, the creative young yearn to be filmmakers rather than novelists. Dallas has become studio and backdrop to a number of commercial film production companies. Television commercials and horror films are ground out at great profit, and occasionally a home-grown syndicate will produce a popular drama for national distribution. But filmmaking in Dallas is not yet art—with one exception: the work of Ken Harrison. This young man, who has a loose association with Channel 13, the public television station, continues to produce documentaries and dramas of a singularly lyric nature. He has received a number of prestigious grants and awards.

There is in Dallas, however, a great appreciation for fine films, as evidenced by the growing reputation of the USA Film Festival, which screens each spring at Southern Methodist University. Begun in 1971, the festival features American-made films and honors a director with a retrospective. In the past, Frank Capra, Joseph Mankiewicz, William Wyler, and Mervyn LeRoy have appeared to discuss their work with fans and critics.

MUSIC

In the late 1880s Hans Kreissig, well trained in piano and conducting, came to Dallas from Germany. Under his direction the Dallas Symphony began in 1900 with thirty-six members, and a first performance was held at Turner Hall. Mr. Kreissig's regime ended in 1905, and Walter Fried conducted the symphony from 1905–11 and then after World War I from 1918–24. The orchestra was still not a professional one, but it became much more so under the direction, from 1925 to 1942, of Paul Van Katwijk, followed by that of Jacques Singer. There was no symphony during World War II, but immediately afterward music came to Dallas with more excitement and more growth than at any other time in its short history. This new vitality was due to the vibrating personality of Antal Dorati, who directed the DSO from 1945–49 and who was committed to making the orchestra one of the finest in the United States. He was given encouragement in Dallas by a group of musical and financial leaders who wanted to place the DSO in the national picture. Under Dorati all members were professional. Local subscriptions grew in number and the city took pride in its music. In 1949 Walter Hendl succeeded Dorati. He had been associate conductor of the New York Philharmonic Orchestra—a strong, demanding musician. Hendl continued as conductor until 1958, when Paul Kletski came for a few years to bring a new spirit of energy and life.

By 1961 George Solti was conductor, with Donald Johannos as musical director. By then the excitement was passing and the DSO was beginning to lose its first flush of glory. Johannos was conductor from 1962–70, followed by Anshel Brusilow from 1970–72. The orchestra reached a low ebb, and its quality and prestige were fast disappearing. It became an orchestra in trouble, one trying to please everyone and really pleasing no one. The last few years have found the DSO plagued with tremendous financial problems. Community members, once so active in the symphony's life, deserted. Support from the business community is essential for the symphony to survive, but artistic control is another matter. A strong musical director, unimpeded by the local well-meaning laymen, is needed to shape and set policy. Recently, Louis Lane was brought in as conductor and remains as co-principal conductor.

There are still a number of smaller musical functions that have been sustained for long periods of time:

THE DALLAS CHAMBER MUSIC SERIES was formed in 1945 by Elmer Scott. Many members of the old Civic Federation of Dallas, which existed as far back as 1913, were active in forming the Chamber Music Series because they wanted professional musicians performing on a regular basis. In 1955 the series was incorporated and is known as the Elmer Scott Concert Series. Five concerts are given each year in Caruth Auditorium on the Southern Methodist University campus, and the quality is very high.

DALLAS CIVIC MUSIC ASSOCIATION was started in 1930 by the push of such businessmen as Eli Sanger, Howard Beasley, Edward Titche, and Christian Weichsel. Basically it used the support and help of its membership to make the series productive.

THE DALLAS GRAND OPERA ASSOCIATION, the organization that brought the Metropolitan Opera to Dallas on a yearly basis, was instigated by Dallas businessman Arthur Kramer, Sr., followed by his son, Arthur Kramer, Jr. Finally, the senior Kramer persuaded the Metropolitan management to come to Dallas, and since 1939, except for a few years' hiatus, it has been an important musical event in the spring of each year. The Dallas business community has underwritten the opera since the beginning, encouraging public support and bringing prestige to Dallas.

THE DALLAS CIVIC OPERA COMPANY was the inspiration of Lawrence Kelly, a native of Chicago, who was encouraged by John Rosenfield to form a civic opera company that would present the best in opera on a professional level. Mr. Kelly came to Dallas in 1957 and until his untimely death in 1974, produced some of the most stimulating grand opera in the United States. The strength of this seventeen-year project is phenomenal. Kelly never hesitated about the need for quality, and quality cost money and know-how; there was always a distinction in his mind between the amateur and the professional.

THE DALLAS COMMUNITY COURSE is a joint effort of Southern Methodist University and Temple Emanu-El. It began in 1938 with the intention of bringing a mixture of popular programs into the area. The series has maintained a well-balanced mixture of lectures, performers, dramas, music, and dance.

Lawrence Kelly.

217

FINE ARTS

As early as 1909, a gallery was available at Fair Park known as the Dallas Public Art Gallery. Edward G. Eisenlohr, a banker who turned to painting and who became one of the directors of the Dallas Art Association, was one of the first people to interest the community in painting. In 1933 a new home was founded in the Dallas Power and Light Building. Finally, in 1936, for the Texas Centennial, a new building was erected to house the Dallas Museum of Fine Arts. Richard Foster Howard was the first trained museum director from 1937–41, followed by Jerry Bywaters from 1942–62, then by Merrill Reuppel from 1963–73, and recently by Harry Parker, formerly of the New York Metropolitan Museum of Art.

One of the interesting art developments occurred in the late 1950s and the 1960s when ten couples formed a Society of Contemporary Art, whose purpose was to relate Dallas more and more closely to the world of living art—to contemporary art. The Dallas Museum of Contemporary Art first presented a showing in a movie theater lobby across from the Melrose Hotel. This was in 1957. By 1959, with Edward Marcus as president, they acquired a building on Cedar Springs that was donated by a number of well-off Dallas citizens.

From 1959 to 1962, the Dallas Museum of Contemporary Art was an exciting and viable force in the community. The opening exhibit in their permanent headquarters was "Signposts of the 20th Century." In 1959 the museum asked Douglas MacAgy, formerly of the Wildenstein Gallery in New York, to become director and curator. For three years there was a tremendous upsurge in contemporary painting and exhibitions. Membership grew to well over 1,700. MacAgy felt that Dallas would be an ideal place for a contemporary museum because of its lack of restraining tradition. He believed that an art museum should be "an institution which stirs, broadens, and deepens the lives of individuals in our society." But by 1963 the Contemporary Museum was in financial trouble, and a merger with the Dallas Museum of Fine Arts was considered. It finally closed its doors in 1964, the collection becoming a part of the Dallas Museum of Fine Arts. Art collectors from all over the country became interested in the Contemporary Museum and contributed outstanding paintings and sculptures. These art works were placed in a separate trust foundation when the museum merged with the Dallas Museum of Fine Arts.

The latest museum in Dallas is the Meadows Museum, housed in the Meadows School of the Arts at Southern Methodist University. This was founded by Algur Meadows in 1965. Dr. William Jordan has been director since 1967. It houses a very fine collection of Spanish paintings of different periods.

While pictorial artists in Dallas had to await the establishment of an appreciative sector of society—patrons who would support studios and galleries and muse-

OVERLEAF, TOP ROW:
Norma Young, Jac Alder. Theatre Three.
Nicola Rescigno, Dallas Civic Opera.
Jerry Bywaters Cochran, dancer-teacher.

SECOND ROW, CENTER:
Louis Lane, conductor, Dallas Symphony.

BOTTOM:
John Lunsford, curator, Dallas Museum of Fine Arts.

ums—writers were not so dependent upon that establishment. For journalists and historians there were the unfolding of a frontier and the growth of an urban culture to record and interpret. This, in the main, has been the role of the writer in Dallas. The refinements of technique of the novelist and poet have been the exception rather than the rule.

Literary work, however, has flourished in Dallas, and publishers have been alert to the varied talents that emerged. Regional Americana was a natural beginning where so much history had occurred to inspire the writer. There were true stories of drama and adventure to be told. There were characters to be caught and held in word pictures. There was an environment and life-style to be described. There was a psychology of society to be studied, understood, articulated. Later and just as naturally the writers extended their work into areas beyond their regional and national boundaries.

Authors in the various categories of fiction and non-fiction include Ramon Adams, John Ardoin, Sam Blair, Benjamin Capps, Helen Corbitt, Paul Crume, Herbert Gambrell, Wayne Gard, A. C. Greene, Leon Harris, Jr., Siddie Jo Johnson, Myra Livingston, Stanley Marcus, Frances Mossiker, Albert Outler, Luise Putcamp, Jr., John William Rogers, Michael Ryan, Blackie Sherrod, Patsy Swank, Emily Weisberg Sunstein, Marshall Terry, Lon Tinkle, Frank X. Tolbert, and Victor White, all of Dallas.

In addition, the local chapter of the Texas Poetry Society has a large and active membership.

Texas, and especially Dallas, has become a new mecca for artists, not so much because of a refined art awareness but rather because this is still, in a sense, virgin frontier where new money and open tastes are eager for aesthetics. Eastern expatriates such as Raffaele Martini and David McCullough, to name but two of many, have found freedom and energy here. Of the older generation, Olin Trevis, Otis Dozier, and Perry Nichols must be named for their importance in teaching as well as for their painting. At ninety-two Clara Williamson is, of course, one of America's most recognized folk painters. Of the middle contemporary generation Roger Winters and David McManaway are justly acclaimed, and the younger generation of artists are numerous, including such talents as George Green, Robert Wade, James Surls, and Juergen Strunck.

DANCE

Dance has always been considered the "stepchild" of the arts and this is true in Dallas. It is only within the past few years that the Dallas Civic Ballet has been given community support for its growth. At present there is a professional company, formed in 1974, as part of the Dallas Civic Ballet Society, but called the Touring

Company. George Skibine has been artistic director since 1969. The original society was formed in 1957 with Mrs. Hubert Foster as president, but it was not until Skibine took over the society in 1969 that a functioning organization began to appear. Mary Heller Sasser has acted as general manager since 1973. Its repertoire leans heavily toward the classics.

Before 1957 many groups were formed. Dance teachers within the community tried to form dance councils which would serve as a "melting pot" for the talent assembled, but none of these groups had consistency or artistic integrity.

Two prominent names in the ballet field need to be mentioned: Edith James, a moving force in the Dallas community from the 1940s until the late 1960s; and Nikita Talin, former soloist with the Ballet Russe de Monte Carlo, who came to Dallas in the 1950s. Both teachers were highly motivated to produce good dance. Alexandra Danilova, prima ballerina with the Ballet Russe de Monte Carlo, became a guest artist with the James School for many years.

A few spurts of dance activity occurred before this. Theodore Kosloff, with a background from the Russian Imperial Ballet School and the Diagaleff Ballet Company, came to Dallas briefly and took the town by storm from 1929 to 1934. Kosloff was a powerful taskmaster who expected excellence from all his students. He gave productions at the Fair Park Music Hall with the Dallas Symphony Orchestra under Van Katwijk.

The early history of Dallas dance can be traced to a Professor George, who, in 1880, began to teach such dances as the schottische, polka, waltz, and quadrille. Mrs. John Priestly Hart took over from Professor George and for twenty-five years dominated the dance scene. But the dance training was all in ballroom dancing. Subsequently, Miss Helen Doty came from the Ziegfield Follies. She was a pupil of Adolph Bolm's, a graduate of the Russian Imperial School, and she was the first to introduce the classical ballet to the region.

Dallas has always been a "ballet" city. *Swan Lake, Sleeping Beauty, Giselle, Les Sylphides,* and *Nutcracker* are especially popular. Representatives of contemporary dance appeared from time to time: Mary Wigman, Harold Kreutzberg, and the Jooss Ballet, followed by Martha Graham and her company in 1946, and Miss Graham as a solo performer with the Dallas Symphony in 1955. But modern dance has never gained a foothold in this part of the country.

Perhaps the community responds more to the traditions of classicism than to the freedom of contemporary movement. It is still too early to tell, for it is only within the past few years that varied action in dance has been taking place. At the moment, dance remains far behind the other performing arts. It is possible, with the national interest in dance growing, that Dallas will respond with more versatility in the 1970s.

At present, Dallas can be compared to an economic abstraction that never finds a meaning. We know that there is a tremendous "potential," but will we realize it? Basically Dallas' very beginning was due to business—the bankers, insurance companies, oil people, cattle industry, real estate brokers, cotton industry, etc. Its very nature does not create an atmosphere for the arts. But the arts have thrived on and off during its 135-year life. Perhaps what is needed are new visionaries—persons willing to push Dallas forward into creative activity. These must be highly motivated and driven persons who believe that the arts are important to the city's spiritual well-being. Such people must have the kind of integrity that produced the arts in the past, not solely for personal gain, but to enrich the community. The arts are relevant to a city's life. If they are forgotten, the soul of the city is lost.

Dallas is constantly emerging as a cultural community, but it has never come into full flowering. Throughout its short history, the expectation of bigger things just ahead has dominated Dallas citizens, but no longer does the reality live up to the expectations.

Pierre Boulez, conductor of the New York Philharmonic, has said, "If you live in the shadow of the past, then you're like a plant hidden from the sun and you just vanish. The vitality of a civilization depends on each generation putting into question the achievements of the past."

Art reflects life, and in this process Dallas tends toward classicism, the accepted and conservative point of view. We don't trust our own judgment. We rely on the "star system," the big names. The arts in Dallas foster pretense. They are not something about which we personally feel strongly; rather we comfortably assume that if something has survived for a long time, it must be good. We don't trust ourselves to know whether what is new is also good, and this is sad. What is important is making the arts part of our life, and this, in the end, will produce true opinions and tastes—and what is more exciting than controversy? But because artistic leadership in Dallas is in transition, hopefully the present situation is only an "intermission" of sorts.

An Ohio farm boy born in 1866, Elmer Scott first came to Dallas as a traveling salesman in 1889. He went to Chicago in 1889 to join the staff of R. W. Sears, of Sears, Roebuck and Company, and returned to Dallas in 1906 to lay the groundwork for the company to open a Dallas branch. Resigning his position in 1913, Mr. Scott remained in Dallas and concentrated on an entirely new career: the establishment of a cultural center for the city. It was called the Civic Federation, and it opened its modest doors in the summer of 1917. Under Elmer Scott's leadership and the support he generated, it grew into national recognition for its key contributions to adult education and social welfare. Few are the arts enjoyed in Dallas now whose seeds were not first planted at the Civic Federation. Mr. Scott died in 1954.

A Dallas native born in 1900, John Rosenfield attended the University of Texas in Austin and Columbia University in New York. He went on the staff of the New York *Evening Mail* as assistant to drama critic Burns Mantle and pioneered in reviewing motion pictures. In New York he married Claire Burger and returned to Dallas in 1923, joining the staff of the Dallas *Morning News* a year later. In 1925 he became the paper's amusements editor and held that post until just prior to his death in 1966. His constructive influence and fame as critic of the performing arts won many honors, among them the Motion Pictures Directors Award as outstanding critic and the Texas Federation of Music Clubs Award for his service to music, notably the establishment of the annual Dealey Awards. He wrote frequently for the New York *Times* and *Theater Arts* and was often a guest on the Metropolitan Opera radio quiz programs. DALLAS MORNING NEWS.

STATE FAIR

One of Texas' most popular writers, A. C. Greene has made Dallas his home and its history his province for twenty years. A native Texan, born in Abilene, Greene served with the marines in the Pacific and China during World War II. He has written for newspapers, magazines, and television, taught history and literature in two universities, and owned his own bookstore. Greene was book editor and editor of the editorial page of the Dallas *Times Herald* until the late sixties, when he turned to writing books, among the most recent, *Dallas: The Deciding Years.*

Power and Politics

by A. C. GREENE

It used to be so simple: Uncle Bob Thornton would make a few phone calls or Mayor Erik Jonsson would have half a dozen other members of the Dallas Citizens Council to lunch at the City Club, and the problem was solved—or answers were furnished, conclusions reached, actions begun. That was community leadership, that was municipal power. Everybody knew who ran Dallas: the business establishment, the decision makers, the oligarchy—call it what you would. Once the pyramid of power (which numbered as few as three at the apex and as many as 250 at the base) was convinced, things moved quickly and (in most cases) smoothly to a foregone conclusion. Of course, there were crises when, pushed by the clock, the calendar, or circumstances, this process didn't allow the broad citizenry in on the action. Accomplishments were announced more often than they were debated. But the decision makers (as one writer named them) figured that was all right. They'd earned the right to trust from those who counted in the community. Scandal, machine politics in City Hall, personal jealousy were not a part of the leadership game. As the newspapers pointed out, these were not only the most powerful but the most dedicated men "for the good of Dallas."

Through the 1940s, the '50s, and most of the '60s it worked that way: a machine that wasn't a machine, an aristocracy that volunteered its service but was absolute in its control. Might was inherited along business lines instead of bloodlines, and all of it based on a sort of gentleman's agreement that no one would grab for private power or overreach for personal gain.

DALLAS CITY COUNCIL 1975

Left to right, Rose Renfro, Bill Nicol, L. A. Murr, Adlene Harrison, Lucy Patterson, Willie Cothrum, Mayor Wes Wise, Richard Smith, Gary Weber, John Leedom.

But now?

By the mid-seventies you had, for one thing, Mayor Wesley Arthur Wise as top elected city official. Not a member of the Citizens Council, not a corporate executive, not wealthy (in fact, one of his greatest political trinkets was a 1966 Volkswagen automobile which was once seized for debts)—not even a businessman. So how did Wes Wise get in office? It proved relatively simple. He got in through a technological innovation that the oligarchy people overlooked, possibly because they owned and controlled it. A well-known sportscaster, Wise slipped into City Hall by way of television identity. He was much better known to the voters than the men who hired and then opposed him. Elected a member of the City Council as an independent in a 1969 upset, Wise soon proved to have the keenest voter identity of any political figure in Dallas, and in 1971 he soundly whipped Avery Mays, a respected establishment figure—backed by the Citizens Council and its city political arm, the Citizens Charter Association—for the mayor's job.

Mayor Robert Folsom. GITTINGS.

Al Lipscomb, South Dallas leader.

Judge George Allen, former mayor pro tem.

It was the first time in decades such a complete "outsider" had hammered his way inside. Earle Cabell had whipped the oligarchy candidate for mayor in 1961, but Cabell, for all his personal independent ways, was "one of us" insofar as the business leaders were concerned. Some of the power structure leaders were scornful, calling Wise "that clown." But the sports announcer had turned into a smart, attractive politician—and in the 1973 mayor's race, no one could be found who wanted to stand up and get creamed by "that clown," so Wise went unopposed.

By election time in 1975, desperation had set in among the old oligarchy. Something had to be done. City Hall was slipping away. Someone of substance with the business imprimatur had to be persuaded to oppose Mayor Wise. There was a scramble—but it was away from the pedestal, not toward it. After a lengthy and uncharacteristically assiduous search for a requisite candidate, John L. Schoell-kopf—who certainly was not cut to the old power pattern—took the bid and was badly defeated, as everyone had presumed he would be. Not only that, but the City Council, elected for the first time partially on a single-member district basis (all places had formerly been voted on by the city at large), slipped from CCA control. The oligarchy, as *the* political force in Dallas affairs, was crippled if not shattered. But the success of Wes Wise, singlehandedly and consecutively defeating the strongest political party in town, was but a symptom. The changing picture of power in Dallas goes deeper than one man or one office. It became clear, by the 1970s, that no matter what things might become, they were never going to go back to being what they were.

Wise, fired by success and, admittedly, needing a bigger salary, resigned early in 1976 to run for Congress, leaving Mayor Pro-tem Adlene Harrison to become Dallas' first woman mayor. Despite indications she could win, she refused to enter the special mayoral election, and former City Councilman Garry Weber and land developer Robert Folsom waged a close and costly campaign between millionaires which saw Folsom win by a hair only after a runoff. Neither had endorsement of the CCA, although Folsom plainly was the oligarchy's favored contender. Weber, initially a CCA council candidate, had won as an independent against CCA candidates in two prior council races. Folsom, an SMU athlete from the Doak Walker era, had been a member of the Dallas Independent School District board and benefited from his stand against "forced" school busing and his association with the business power structure. As mayor, his image goes back to Dallas of the 1950s and '60s, and he has declared he wants no further public office.

On the surface, the bare fact of Folsom's victory tended to make some wonder if, indeed, Wise had been a fluke, that perhaps the change in the wind was a false forecast. The conditions still hold, however. The Folsom-Weber battle was bitter and perhaps more divisive than decisive. Almost half of Dallas went against the establishment, gave it a fight that was clear indication of things to come. Preston Jones's play comes to mind. The old way had hung on, but it looked more and more like *The Last Meeting of the Knights of the White Magnolia.*

Federal Judge Sarah Hughes.

To understand the way Dallas was run, we need to set up a short history course. For most of the time between the late 1930s and the late 1960s, Dallas was run, as a city, by members of that organization already mentioned, the Dallas Citizens Council. It was more like a board of directors than an executive panel—but its power lacked no degree of effectiveness. The group was first brought to national attention in 1949 with a lengthy feature in *Fortune* magazine titled, "The Dydamic Men of Dallas"—an article that, far from questioning its role, dwelt on the astonishing success and ease of the Citizens Council in developing Dallas' business interests. But later, during the time of the assassination of President John F. Kennedy and its aftermath, world attention was again focused on the organization—this time with unflattering emphasis as "the Dallas oligarchy." Even *Fortune,* once so enthusiastic over these "dydamic leaders," hinted that as "the oligarchy" they might compose a dictatorship. And more than one media reporter hinted at sinister manipulations and democratic disregards.

But the Dallas Citizens Council was not (and is not) a myth, or some booger-bear that hides by day and prowls by night. It is merely a corporation chartered by the state of Texas in 1937 "to study, confer and act upon any matter, civic or economic in character, which may be deemed to affect the welfare of the city of Dallas." No tricky subclauses, no legal gobbledygook or secret handshakes. A closed member-

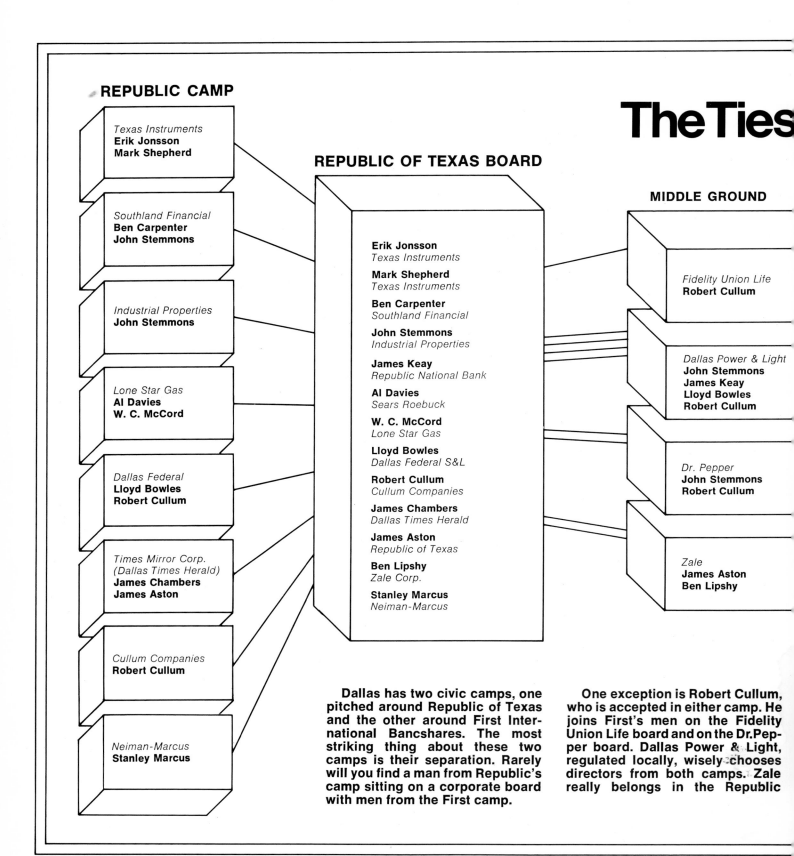

REPUBLIC CAMP

Texas Instruments
Erik Jonsson
Mark Shepherd

Southland Financial
Ben Carpenter
John Stemmons

Industrial Properties
John Stemmons

Lone Star Gas
Al Davies
W. C. McCord

Dallas Federal
Lloyd Bowles
Robert Cullum

Times Mirror Corp.
(Dallas Times Herald)
James Chambers
James Aston

Cullum Companies
Robert Cullum

Neiman-Marcus
Stanley Marcus

REPUBLIC OF TEXAS BOARD

Erik Jonsson
Texas Instruments

Mark Shepherd
Texas Instruments

Ben Carpenter
Southland Financial

John Stemmons
Industrial Properties

James Keay
Republic National Bank

Al Davies
Sears Roebuck

W. C. McCord
Lone Star Gas

Lloyd Bowles
Dallas Federal S&L

Robert Cullum
Cullum Companies

James Chambers
Dallas Times Herald

James Aston
Republic of Texas

Ben Lipshy
Zale Corp.

Stanley Marcus
Neiman-Marcus

The Ties

MIDDLE GROUND

Fidelity Union Life
Robert Cullum

Dallas Power & Light
John Stemmons
James Keay
Lloyd Bowles
Robert Cullum

Dr. Pepper
John Stemmons
Robert Cullum

Zale
James Aston
Ben Lipshy

Dallas has two civic camps, one pitched around Republic of Texas and the other around First International Bancshares. The most striking thing about these two camps is their separation. Rarely will you find a man from Republic's camp sitting on a corporate board with men from the First camp.

One exception is Robert Cullum, who is accepted in either camp. He joins First's men on the Fidelity Union Life board and on the Dr. Pepper board. Dallas Power & Light, regulated locally, wisely chooses directors from both camps. Zale really belongs in the Republic

That Bind

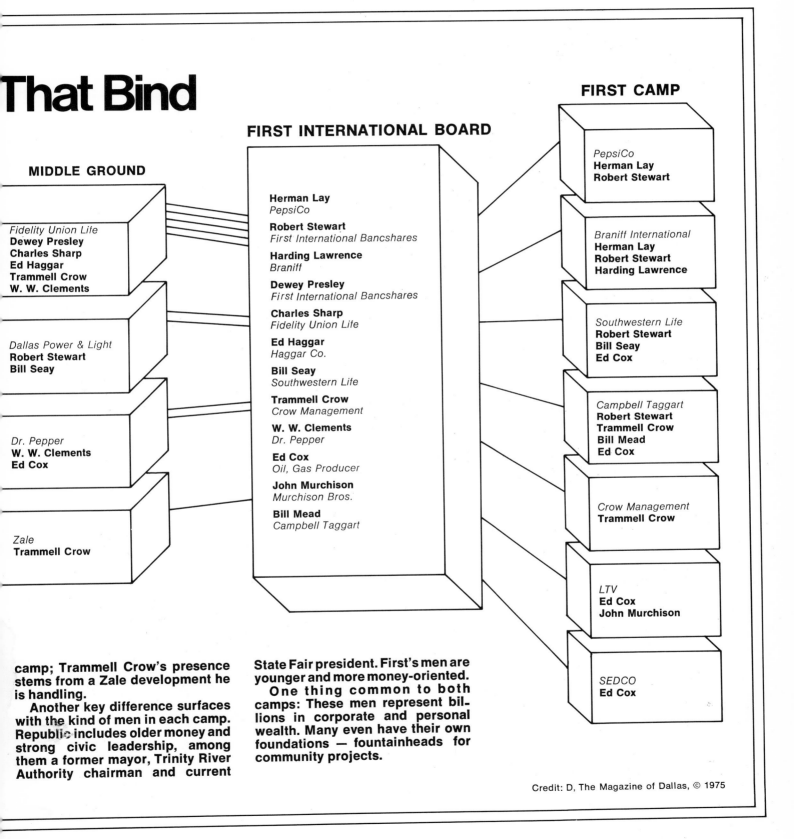

FIRST CAMP

MIDDLE GROUND

Fidelity Union Life
Dewey Presley
Charles Sharp
Ed Haggar
Trammell Crow
W. W. Clements

Dallas Power & Light
Robert Stewart
Bill Seay

Dr. Pepper
W. W. Clements
Ed Cox

Zale
Trammell Crow

FIRST INTERNATIONAL BOARD

Herman Lay
PepsiCo

Robert Stewart
First International Bancshares

Harding Lawrence
Braniff

Dewey Presley
First International Bancshares

Charles Sharp
Fidelity Union Life

Ed Haggar
Haggar Co.

Bill Seay
Southwestern Life

Trammell Crow
Crow Management

W. W. Clements
Dr. Pepper

Ed Cox
Oil, Gas Producer

John Murchison
Murchison Bros.

Bill Mead
Campbell Taggart

PepsiCo
Herman Lay
Robert Stewart

Braniff International
Herman Lay
Robert Stewart
Harding Lawrence

Southwestern Life
Robert Stewart
Bill Seay
Ed Cox

Campbell Taggart
Robert Stewart
Trammell Crow
Bill Mead
Ed Cox

Crow Management
Trammell Crow

LTV
Ed Cox
John Murchison

SEDCO
Ed Cox

camp; Trammell Crow's presence stems from a Zale development he is handling.

Another key difference surfaces with the kind of men in each camp. Republic includes older money and strong civic leadership, among them a former mayor, Trinity River Authority chairman and current State Fair president. First's men are younger and more money-oriented.

One thing common to both camps: These men represent billions in corporate and personal wealth. Many even have their own foundations — fountainheads for community projects.

ship, true (you have to be invited to join), and no public meetings—but it's worked long and worked well. It was a system unique to Dallas among larger American cities, this voluntary political machine that governed and directed community life through its detached but firmly controlled management units.

The most public of these units is the CCA, the city political party by which it elected 95 per cent of the City Council members and all but the two aforementioned mayors during its days of decision. Another arm, the Committee for Good Schools, saw to it that acceptable school board members were elected—and save for a couple of later years, the CGS was even more successful than the CCA. Even the United Way (Fund) campaign took direct oversight from the Citizens Council—and still does. Needless to say, when the state legislators were elected on a county-wide basis, the Citizens Council picked both the legislature slate and the state senators—and, while shunning party politics, wielded tremendous influence in the election of congressmen. In order to hold down partisan ambitions, direct management of municipal business was put in the hands of a city manager, who was named by the City Council, which, in effect, gave the oligarchy a direct voice in his selection and his subsequent acts. (There were no rebels among the Dallas city managers; in fact, several of them went directly to work for major Dallas businesses when they retired from City Hall.) As a further inducement to keeping city government within the bounds of a gentleman's agreement, the mayor and council members drew token pay of only fifty dollars per meeting, and CCA councilmen were to serve only two terms. Thus, the Citizens Council, or one of its various arms, yes-or-noed all civic fund drives and advised-and-consented every municipal decision involving more than a few hundred dollars or a handful of people. The newspapers went along because the people who ran the newspapers were themselves hearty supporters of the council and its political arm. This, with its board room method of operation, protected the Citizens Council from potential opponents and from the mistakes of its agents. Defenders insisted the Citizens Council itself did none of this—that its members, acting as individuals, performed the feats. Critics quoted Shakespeare: . . . a rose by any other name. . . .

The Dallas Citizens Council was the brainchild of a nimble-minded, under-educated (sixth grade), self-made banker named Robert Lee Thornton, who toward the end of his life served three terms as mayor and came to be affectionately known as "Uncle Bob." Thornton, who had come to Dallas as a young man straight from a Texas cotton farm, performed miracles in 1936 by persuading the state to designate Dallas the site for the great Texas Centennial Exposition. Dallas: which didn't have the Alamo like San Antonio, or San Jacinto Battlefield like Houston. Dallas: which wasn't even in existence when Texas won independence from Mexico, the occasion the centennial celebrated. The international publicity—millions of visitors spending millions of dollars in the depths of the Depression—helped lay the foundations for the legendary Big D.

Seeing what consensus could do—Thornton having assembled the cream of Dallas business leadership to back his centennial efforts—the banker called on two of his bigger rivals, Fred Florence at Republic National and Nathan Adams at First National, and laid out his plan for a tight little body of yes-and-no men who could move quickly when opportunity popped up—board chairmen or presidents of locally owned or based big, big businesses—explaining, in the cotton-path grammar that was his trademark, "We didn't have time for no proxy people . . . what we needed was men who could give you boss talk." And it didn't take long for boss power to fill all the vacuums and empty spaces of city control.

The Dallas Citizens Council has always had some 250 members, but from its beginning—with the three big bankers—there was an effective, if informal, guiding force of about twenty men and an even smaller circle of indispensables numbering six or seven. But power had ground rules: you didn't use it to compete, you co-operated "for the good of Dallas." (If it also helped your business, fine—but you couldn't get greedy.) Wealth was taken for granted and autonomous power, as Thornton indicated. But giving of your time was often as important as giving of your money. Few "poor folks" could take off three months to run a United Way campaign, or two years to be mayor. And it was imperative that you head a large enough business to marshal a civic army for drives and projects.

Basically, the oligarchy represented institutions. The chief executive officers of Republic and First National joined the pinnacle regardless of who they were; the head of Dallas Power and Light became an automatic, and so did the newspaper publishers. The top men at Lone Star Gas and Southwestern Bell were offered the top leadership option, and the head men in Dallas for Sears and for Sanger-Harris were never strangers to the top. (Note that all these institutions kept huge amounts of money in their bank accounts and had enormous manpower handy.) Individuals, such as Thornton, or Robert Cullum (Tom Thumb food stores) and Stanley Marcus (Neiman-Marcus), rose to the upper circle through sheer individuality—but they also headed big, local institutions. It is ironic that when Uncle Bob Thornton died in 1964 his individual dominance was not passed along to the institution he founded, Mercantile National Bank.

OVERLEAF: Victor Lallier painting of Dallas leaders, 1951–56, which hangs on the stage of the Republic National Bank auditorium. Back row left to right: B. F. McLain, J. Woodall Rodgers, Dean Robert G. Storey, Fred Florence, John E. Mitchell, Jr., Dr. Edward H. Cary, R. L. Thornton, Sr. Front row left to right: Dr. David Lefkowitz, Judge William H. Atwell, Dr. Umphrey Lee, Karl Hoblitzelle, Nathan Adams, Tom Gooch, John W. Carpenter. COURTESY OF REPUBLIC NATIONAL BANK OF TEXAS.

B. F. McLAIN   J. WOODALL RODGERS   DEAN ROBT. G. STOREY   FRED F. FLORENCE
Dr. DAVID LEFKOWITZ   JUDGE WM. H. ATWELL   Dr. UMPHREY LEE   KARL H

OHN E. MITCHELL, JR.   DR. EDW. H. CARY   R.L. (BOB) THORNTON

ZELLE   NATHAN ADAMS   TOM C. GOOCH   JOHN W. CARPENTER

Born in Manchester, England, in 1859, George Bannerman Dealey sailed from Liverpool with his family in 1870 to Galveston and at fifteen went to work as office boy for Colonel A. H. Belo and his Galveston *News,* which had been founded when the state was a republic. Young Dealey rose rapidly on the staff, and after marrying Olivia Allen, of Lexington, Missouri, he came to Dallas in 1885 to launch the Dallas *Morning News.* From then until his death in 1946 the integrity and dedication of his career as a newspaper publisher made history, plus his leadership in city planning and the many civic causes and philanthropies that held his personal interest. The heritage of his example has been carried forward consistently by his son, E. M. (Ted) Dealey, and by his grandson, Joe M. Dealey, now president of the Dallas *Morning News.* DALLAS MORNING NEWS.

Edwin J. Kiest was born in 1861 in Cook County, Illinois. As a ten-year-old boy he worked in Chicago selling newspapers. He became a printer and rose to an executive with the Western Newspaper Union, which sent him to Dallas as branch manager in 1890. Here he married Elizabeth Patterson Lyon and took over the Dallas *Times Herald* in 1896. To meet the payroll of the struggling little paper of some two thousand circulation, he often pawned his gold watch on Saturday. In later years of success he led support for the city to open the first radio station in the state, WRR, in 1920. Still later he bought radio station KRLD for his newspaper. Mr. Kiest gave outstanding support to the municipal parks system, the State Fair of Texas in Dallas, and Texas A&M University. He died in 1941. DALLAS TIMES HERALD.

When Julius Schepps died in 1971, he was referred to as "the hands of Dallas . . . hands that built . . . hands that reached out to help. . . . Brotherhood was his name."

The man who became and remains legendary was born in St. Louis, Missouri, in 1895 and came to Dallas in 1901 with his Russian refugee parents, who baked and sold bread for their living. He was their delivery boy. Then he delivered newspapers and attended Texas A&M on a basketball scholarship.

After newspaper work in El Paso where he married Phyllis Eickman, Mr. Schepps returned to Dallas to operate the family bakery with his brother George. When that was sold, he went into the insurance business, and later the Schepps Wholesale Liquor Company was organized. As a director of the Mercantile National Bank, his close friendship with R. L. Thornton, Sr., led him into the full spectrum of civic service. Giving became his way of life, personally and materially. No charitable cause was without his leadership. A grateful city, state, and country honored him in every way possible for his Lincolnesque "charity for all."
COURTESY OF THE JEWISH COMMUNITY CENTER.

Several men who would have seemed eligible for key leadership positions in Dallas never got the offer or never wanted local power. The late H. L. Hunt, who was thought by outsiders to have enormous influence in running Dallas, never did. Few oilmen ever did, in fact. Hunt was a loner, not a team player, and besides, the oligarchy was concerned over what many considered his excessively conservative views. Hunt's family, emerging strongly since his death, will probably write a different chapter to that story.

H. Ross Perot, the computer software success, has remained an outsider to the intimacies of the establishment. Perot, too, is a loner, operating nationally and not tied to Dallas. Besides, he was said to bank in California—as one recalls that the Citizens Council was a banker's creation and remained primarily a bankers' club. Jim Ling, who gave conglomerates a Dallas definition, was still waiting to be ushered into the sanctum when his corporate control fell apart. And Clint Murchison, Jr., while as wealthy and dynamic a Dallasite as one could ask for, became *persona non grata* to the oligarchy (a rare instance) when he pulled his professional football team, the Dallas Cowboys, out of the Cotton Bowl and traipsed off to Irving to locate Texas Stadium. The State Fair Association, which owns and operates the Cotton Bowl, is sacrosanct to the power elite—and Irving, despite its proximity, isn't Dallas.

The long Citizens Council-CCA reign had plenty of virtues. First, City Hall was clean, with minimal scandal even among the lower ranks of municipal bureaucracy. Second, organized crime, of the Mafia stripe, did not gain a hold on Dallas. Crimes of passion, too frequent perhaps—but there is no criminal underworld network with its fingers in politics, unions, and city affairs. Dallas was run efficiently if unimaginatively, just the way one might expect a board of directors to run a basic commodities corporation. Dallas also escaped some of the woes of other American cities, despite its zeal for unlimited growth, and has not yet suffered race riots or sullen bitterness among its minorities. As expressed before, there was little to condemn in oligarchy members as individuals. They were (and are) mostly well liked, honest, and honorable, devoted to their concept of Dallas' welfare.

But the Citizens Council made plenty of mistakes during its period at the helm, too. The biggest was in its composition: no teachers, historians, artists, preachers, entertainers, designers, composers, philosophers, professional men, blacks, chicanos, housewives—in fact, no women at all. It was poetic justice, perhaps, that one of the toughest 1975 council races the CCA lost was to Rose Renfroe, an Oak Cliff woman who could never have even gotten one of the oligarchy's big six to return a phone call, back when everybody knew who ran Dallas.

They were sins of ignorance and wrongheadedness: failure to foresee and respond to the sweeping social changes of our age, failure to take into account the "have-nots" as having rights, failure to accept the fact early on that federal aid is essential to running a modern metropolis. Back in the 1950s there was too much tolerance for politicians like Bruce Alger, who, as congressman, cut off Dallas and

"What you keep is what you use, but what you give is what you have" are words at the core of Mrs. Pearl C. Anderson's philosophy as a civic leader and philanthropist, the first woman named honorary lifetime member of the Dallas Chapter of American Red Cross board of directors.

Born in Winn Parish, Louisiana, in 1898, a black girl too poor to have shoes or a school slate, she drew her ABCs on the ground with a stick. But she managed to become a schoolteacher and came to Dallas in 1919. Now she has an honorary doctor of laws degree from Bishop College, where a women's dormitory bears her name.

Mrs. Anderson has served on the board of directors of the United Fund, the Lighthouse for the Blind, and Dallas Day Nursery Association among her many welfare activities, which to her are as personal as her sense of civic and human fellowship.

Dallasites from the twentieth century—and while he received no open support from the Citizens Council, no leader spoke out against his views. The oligarchy's dependence on a "friendly" press, with its lack of criticism and resistance to challenging ideas, blinded the leadership to the need for evaluation and outside judgment. Thus the oligarchy was ill prepared for world reaction to such a cataclysm as the assassination of President Kennedy, and couldn't muster up some essential critical self-examination. Dallas, as a human gathering place, suffered unnecessarily.

Partly from the above and partly through the materialistic criteria of any business-oriented control, Dallas developed an indifference to human needs in its zeal to follow Uncle Bob's exhortation, "Keep th' dirt flyin'!" And although the Citizens Council did order the desegregation of Dallas businesses in a series of get-tough meetings early in the sixties, it had let a stubborn and shortsighted school administration drag its feet and resist racial integration long after resistance was seen to be futile and wasteful and dangerous. But the greatest weakness of oligarchy control is simply that it is not democratic. It does not respond to the needs of all of the people. What's good for Dallas business is not always good for Dallas. The Citizens Council is the continuation of a nineteenth-century idea—colonialism at home—created by men who were literally, in some cases, products of the frontier. It came into being at a time of economic emergency that skirted disaster: the Great Depression. Survival, not style, was its key to civic projects, and anything smacking of the arts and aesthetics was turned over to the ladies. The Citizens Council took political control of a town of some 275,000 persons, many of whom, in those days, were not taken into consideration by any step in decision making. Today that's one-fourth the number of persons in greater Dallas. Dallas long ago transcended its old Texas parameters and must compete with and compare itself to the world—yet the Citizens Council remained the same closed 1937 corporation with the same number of members and the same requirements for membership. While the oligarchy has not been brought to the brink of dissolution and dysfunction, the role of leadership changed because the needs changed—and the needs changed because Dallas changed.

What ended the domination of Dallas by the decision makers? For one thing, the federal courts put an end to most at-large elections, starting with state senatorial districts and ultimately including even school boards. Thus, the most potent political weapon of the establishment—huge campaign funds supporting an entire slate of candidates—was blunted. With single-member districts, it meant independent politicians could build individual power bases in their own sections or among their own social or racial groups and not have to spend thousands of dollars in a fruitless effort to sell voters in far-flung districts that would never vote for them. Single-member districts also mean that in certain areas black or chicano voters will always be dominant—and the Citizens Council and the CCA were late making room for black and brown faces at the political table. On top of all that, the isolated, insulated control group, inaccessible to those it controls, has become an anachronism, whether its powers are benevolent or repressive. New power sectors—blacks, browns, poor, women, the unrepresented at all levels—have created a leadership potential that a strictly business group denies.

An unexpected shift in Texas banking laws brought a sudden change in Dallas power also. Since 1970 an impossible turn has been taken: the big Dallas banks are no longer Dallas banks. They are now Texas banks, part of the newly allowed state-wide bank holding corporations. Local politics, even in Dallas, are too small and might hurt the broader corporation. Besides, Dallas has grown too big to have consensus among business institutions, which are basically competitive. National and international market requirements and opportunities have eroded the strength of local decisions as well as the need. Such massive local undertakings as the Dallas–Fort Worth airport—the last "grand design" of the old leadership group— can't be brought off without opposition in the future, and, as in the case of Southwest Airlines, even small local businesses can't be made to fit the pattern by the shadow government as they once could. There was a time, not many years ago, when even the local court decisions seemed to go automatically with the decisions already made by the power structure.

Finally, there was no genealogy of power within the Citizens Council. As the dominant figures of its beginning died off or retired, no new leaders were readied to sit in the seats of the mighty. For one thing, most of those older civic titans were self-made, reluctant to groom a replacement, or convinced no replacement was possible. For another thing, the times that sustained an oligarchy's leadership passed with a suddenness that denied the opportunity for succession. Besides, leadership is hard to pass along and nearly impossible to train. The Dallas Assembly, formed in 1962 as a training school by the oligarchy, never gained even a fraction of the original's weight—and subsequent "leadership seminars" turned into a weak joke. The heirs never seemed to want the job.

But power, like nature, abhors a vacuum, and if the oligarchy has faltered, leadership must keep going: someone or something will fill the gap. What can Dallas expect?

Too big a segment of Dallas has been without a voice, and this won't continue. Those with no say want to say something, even if it's foolish; those with questions will find a place to ask them, even if they don't believe the answers. The overlooked parts of town are beginning to be heard—and answered—at the single-member ballot box. Dallas leadership is inevitably turning political: elected, not self-appointed. This will probably mean party politics will come to City Hall—whether in the form of national parties or local divisions based on local affiliations. The CCA, after its 1975 disasters, began a reshaping program that could free it from Citizens Council control without cutting off all the council's financial and other assets.

Mondays at City Hall. Council in session.

Running the city of Dallas will be changed from an amateur's part-time hobby to a professional's full-time vocation. Dallas can't afford the luxury of a fifty-dollar-per-week mayor, and by 1975 the City Council members were already demanding more funds for operating their full-time offices. Big-city mayor is the hottest political job in the United States today. The mayor of Dallas has a bigger task than some state governors. With a salary commensurate with a congressman's, the office could attract imaginative, powerful, not honorary, job seekers—persons answering to the voters, not a society of peers; persons to whom the voters can present the bill if time comes to pay for a mistake. You simply couldn't expect that with most of the oligarchy mayors, no matter how fine or wise they were as private citizens. This change to a politicized mayor's office probably means Dallas will also recognize it has outgrown the city manager—an office that answers to the City Council but not to the electorate.

A politicized city hall is not always as neat or as effective as with consensus leadership. The business oligarchy, especially in the days when Dallas was smaller, and more unified in its views—needing economic inputs at a high level and a massive rate—did a better job of developing a city than a political party system might have done. But politics is where leadership comes from in a democracy, and leadership today implies both responsibility and visibility. In Dallas leadership of the future—a future that is already here—there must be "outs" to keep tabs on the "ins." There were few alternatives to the self-appointed decision makers of the forties, fifties, and sixties, no matter how honorable they were. That won't be the case again.

"Oligarchy to anarchy," one old-guard leader mused aloud in 1974, casting a cold eye on the future he could sense was overwhelming him. The fact that he smiled when he said it didn't strip the dismay from his voice.

And after decades of smooth, effective direction from the summit, any widening control probably seemed just that.

The City as Symbol
The Road vs. the Hearth

by BILL PORTERFIELD

The contradictions of man—those that he comes by and those that he creates—have had a heady and heavy hand in the story of Dallas.

Restlessness and fascination for frontier brought men to the forks of the Trinity. The opposite attraction of community kept them here to make a settlement.

This double nature was never more evident than in the character of the founder, John Neely Bryan. He never really decided whether he was coming or going. It is telling that we have Bryan's cabin—the first house in Dallas—but we don't have his bones. Restless in body as well as in spirit, he went to a lost grave.

Bryan and his followers were able to act out their adventurous urges because of the horse and the oxen and the wheel. Man has always been a mover. One way or the other we are going to get there. This urge to go farther and faster is what separated us from those bandy-legged apes of the African savanna. The apes had a lot going for them—plenty of hostility and hunger and territorial imperative—but the ground kept rising up to hit them in the face, so they kept pretty much to the trees. The mantle of man was not bestowed until about a half million years ago when an adventurous Latin by the name of *Pithecanthropus erectus* actually stood erect and walked without the aid of his arms. That, it seems, was the beginning of man's mobility, and it is amazing to consider how the Latins have monopolized our great pioneering voyages. After *Pithecanthropus* came Marco Polo, Christopher Columbus, Ferdinand Magellan. Columbus seems to have taken his inspiration from the adventures of Marco Polo. In his travels about the Far East, Polo rode camels, elephants, stags, dog sleds. Years before he would set sail for the New World, a young Christopher Columbus got a Latin version of Polo's travels and jotted down seventy notes in the margins.

But this is, really, late history. Primitive man had such a foot fetish it took him 400,000 years and quite a few corns to figure out it was easier to ride than walk. Along about 7000 B.C., he hitched up a sled to his woman and made her pull it. When she complained, he explained that he had to keep his arms free for fighting off robbers. It wasn't long before the woman got smart and turned up a tame ox or two to drag the burden. After that, somebody thought up the wheel and added it, and the sled became a wagon, and ruts roads.

But to every journey there is an end, or at least a respite. One stops for the night and looks for food and shelter and perhaps companions. Conversation and goods are traded. A campfire becomes an outpost, the outpost a settlement.

Surely cities are almost as old as the social instinct in man. They grew out of villages and not as haphazardly as we might think. Many ancient cities were built from definite plans. The earliest handwriting we can read is hieroglyphic, and this was the ancient Egyptians' symbol for city:

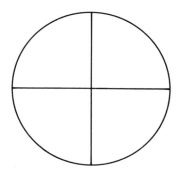

The cross represented the convergence of roads which brought together men and merchandise and ideas. The circle indicated a moat or a wall, as protection against invaders, and it also symbolized unity and a sense of community.

One can see how the ancient Egyptians' symbol for city actually became a pattern for the design of future towns and cities. I suppose it was an unconscious adaptation, if there is such a thing, but it is interesting to see how the same impulses and ideas work in men worlds apart.

The fundamental feature of Babylon, Nineveh, and the ancient cities of Greece and China was the geographical grid with a public square at its center. How do you make a grid? Well, start with the hieroglyphic cross, two main streets intersecting, and then add parallel streets until you have the grid.

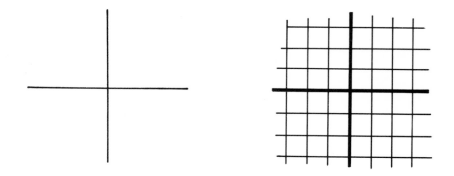

ABOVE: Main Street, 1891. ROGERS PHOTOS.

This was exactly the plan of Thurii, which Pericles founded about 443 B.C. Pericles was supposed to have consulted the Delphic Oracle about the proper site for Thurii, and the Oracle replied with a riddle:

"You must found your city where you shall drink water by measure and eat barley cakes without measure."

Well, they found a spring called Medimnos, which meant measure, so that's where they built, on the Tarentum Gulf along the trade route to Sicily. The architect was Hippodamus, and he was very proud of his plan for Thurii. But we can see that he was derivative rather than original. Thurii, incidentally, flourished until about 188 B.C., when it became a military outpost of Rome.

But copying from the past is part of the practice we call civilization. There was really nothing new in the initial designs of Dallas or Johnson City or Stephenville. Grid plan, later a courthouse replacing the fountain and temple of old. Just as there was really nothing new in Erik Jonsson's Goals for Dallas. In 600 B.C. Alcaeus, the Greek poet and friend of Sappho, wrote: "Not houses finely roofed or the stones of walls well-builded, nay, nor canals and dockyards make the city, but men able to use their opportunity." What do we hear, 2,570 years later, but this from Erik Jonsson: "More important, though, than any visible achievements, is the greater understanding by the people of the city's problems and its opportunities."

What of our problems as a community?

Mobility sticks in my mind. It has been both a blessing and a hindrance, a technological magnification of our motives and manners. As Americans acquired more mobility, shifting from beasts to machines, Dallas grew accordingly. We were a town before the railroads came to make us a city. The airlines put us within hours of the rest of the world.

But it was the automobile—that uppermost symbol of the modern individual's mobility—that carried Dallas and the rest of the country into the twentieth century. With the coming of the car, America and Americans would never be the same. No longer removed from one another by distance and bad roads and the insularity of country ways and traditions, we came to town and congregated in the citites.

It is ironic that the conveyance that helped bring us together to make Dallas spurt in population has now become the means for flight to the suburbs and a diminution of the city proper.

Dallas is one of the most racially segregated metropolises in the United States, and the automobile has allowed whites to widen their distance from blacks and browns. We integrate on the television screen and we integrate in hotels and restaurants and ball parks, and more and more we integrate at work as well as at play. But we do not mix in our housing. Downtown Dallas has become a commercial honeycomb for workers by day, an empty hive by night. Affluence has followed the whites to the suburbs, draining the city itself of the buoyancy of a sound tax base. The city proper began to lose population, for the first time, in 1973. The poor and the minorities remain in the middle, victims of unemployment and absentee landlords as well as the police, who act as sentries on the border between the haves and the have-nots. The schools are becoming blacker as whites leave. Federal attempts to bring the races together have not been successful. Some progress has been made in giving blacks and browns a voice in local government, but the great economic and social gulf has not been bridged. In this, of course, Dallas is not unique, except in certain degrees. Its lack of an efficient and far-reaching mass transit system has kept the poor in their place and reinforced the segregation. The bus system is inadequate. The only way to get around Dallas is by car, and in an exaggerated social sense, the spirit that propels the rush-hour traffic homeward is one of retreat into one's own kind.

But this has always been so, even in horse and buggy days. The automobile simply makes the impulse easier, while at the same time radically changing the old attitudes toward community. In a sprawling Metroplex where classes and races confine themselves to kind and kin, the sense of a single whole community is weakened. As Warren Leslie has pointed out, Dallas is at least "five cities in the middle of nowhere."

And yet, conversely, the technology of transportation and mass communication has also allowed us to maintain at least a symbolic oneness. We all identify with the Dallas Cowboys from Irving. We all watch Iola Johnson on Channel 8. We all take pride in Charley Pride and Lee Trevino. There are many such symbols that speak to us of community and draw us together.

The foremost symbol is the downtown skyline.

We all look to it as our landmark. It is true we do not use it as we once did, as the only and actual center of our commerce. Most of us shop in the suburbs now. But we use it nonetheless. In spite of the sprawl away from downtown, the men behind the big banks and business institutions have committed themselves and their companies to remain at the core, at the heart of the city. And one can see a heartening renewal taking place. The great gleaming office towers continue to rise. And developers have returned to the inner city with such provocative projects as Reunion, Thanksgiving Square, the subterranean shopping center that began beneath One Main Place, and the Warehouse Historical District. The splendid new City Hall fronts the Convention Center, and to the immediate east old Fair Park promises to become not only the seat of the Cotton Bowl and State Fair and Music Hall and museums, but a recreational and cultural attraction the year round. Town Lake is a useful and aesthetic possibility. With all these inducements intertwined and connected by esplanades and walk paths and transit systems, downtown Dallas will, like William Faulkner's generic Man, "not only endure but prevail."

In spite of Sodom and Gomorrah and Babylon and its scarlet women, in spite of riots in Detroit and bankruptcy in New York, the city has always been the highest expression of man's civilization. It is the seat of the temple, the market, the hall of justice, the academy of learning, the museum of the arts. Romans saw their cities as the peak of human evolution. Why, a king without a city was unthinkable. Arthur

Last Run of a Dallas Street Car — Jany 1956

OPPOSITE, ABOVE: Opening of Central Expressway, August 14, 1956, which took nine years to complete. Attending were all mayors who had served to that date: George Sargent, W. M. Holland, J. B. Adoue, Jr., R. L. Thornton, Sr., Woodall Rodgers, Wallace Savage. COURTESY OF R. L. THORNTON, JR.

OPPOSITE, BELOW: Last run of a Dallas streetcar, 1956. Passengers include Jerome Crossman, then president of the Chamber of Commerce, R. L. Thornton, Sr., William R. Burns, of Dallas Transit Company. COURTESY OF R. L. THORNTON, JR.

ABOVE: Luxury haven for the turn-of-the-century traveler, the Oriental Hotel in downtown Dallas.

had to have his Camelot, Peter the Great his St. Petersburg. Civilization, it is clear from the Latin meaning of the word, is what goes on in cities. So we had Zion, the city of God.

Thoreau himself was only a hermit for a day. He spent less than two years on Walden Pond, out of the forty-five that he lived. He had to go back to Concord to have his book published and to make a living.

One suspects that cities have not always been the noxious clots some American cities have become. The ancient Greeks kept their city-states small and arcadian, and if Athens got too crowded they didn't add on to it, but sent a colony out to found a new town several miles away. Massive, monumental Rome became the Eternal City because of a stability in design that outlasted the Holy Empire. Since then all the world's great cities have been different, as unique as the people who built them. But the common characteristic of Amsterdam and Paris, of St. Petersburg and London and Washington, is that they were laid out as living works of art, subject to growth and change, but not thrown up and tacked onto. Sir Kenneth Clark has said that New York was built "to the glory of Mammon—money, gain, the new god of the nineteenth century." But one feels the same revulsion for Los Angeles, for different reasons. There the unchecked impulses are horizontal rather than vertical. A twentieth-century city, still hounded by materialism, still indifferent to aesthetics and the grace of grass and trees, but, because of the automobile, more sprawling than spiraling in its run for the money.

Are we back to the barbaric? Have human values been lost in a relentless vulgarity of concrete and neon and tract housing which threatens to stretch across the country and meld into strip cities, one indistinguishable from the other, whether you're in Houston or Hoboken?

A few years ago, *Fortune* magazine brought together a conference of city planners, and they predicted that Americans will "soon be living in 15 or 20 great strip cities, which will be neither rural or urban but an abomination. Almost everyone will have to commute to work."

The irony, and it is a beautiful one, is that in spite of their predictions, each and every one of those enlightened planners is working against what he considers the inevitable. Other men of vision have joined them. Perhaps . . .

Cities, like nations, rise and fall, but man somehow abides. Down in the jungles of Brazil, a complete new city was built in 1960. This was Brasília, the capital. It was four years in the making. There was a national contest for the layout of the new city, and the architect, Lucio Costa, was the winner. Here is what he came up with:

A cross, a Christian cross:

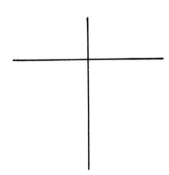

If we draw a circle around it, to symbolize unity and community, we see how closely it resembles the oldest symbol we know for city—the ancient Egyptian hieroglyphic.

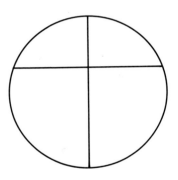

OPPOSITE: The Dallas–Fort Worth Regional Airport.

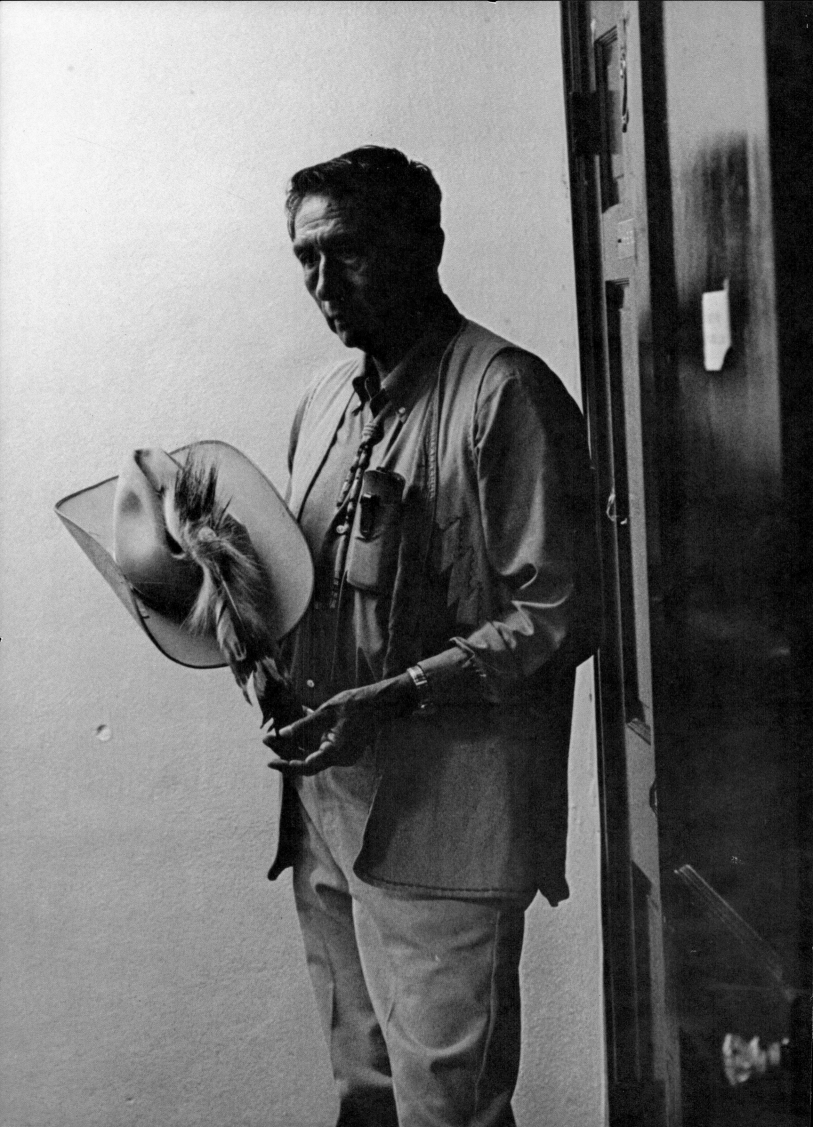

Return of the Natives

by EVELYN OPPENHEIMER

As in all life cycles, at the end we go back to the beginning. In any part of America this means the people who were here first, the native American Indian whose race barely survived conquest and barely escaped genocide.

In Texas the first history was recorded in Indian pictographs which have been found all the way from the Rio Grande to the Panhandle.

In the Dallas area eastward there were mainly the Caddo tribes, among them the Wichitas from the Red River southward to the Waco area. Their culture is another lost treasure among many, as we dig now to rediscover what was destroyed.

Today the descendants of the Indian heritage of many tribes throughout the Southwest have come to Dallas, thousands of men and women and their children. Like all minority groups, they are engaged in seeking the opportunities that their fathers lacked—the chance to learn, to work, to live, and to give of themselves to the city of their choice in this country, which, in the very deepest sense of the word to the Indian, is home.